# I BELIEVE

# I BELIEVE

## Stories of Faith from
## *Saga* Magazine

### THORA HIRD
### WITH ELIZABETH GORT

Fount
*An Imprint of HarperCollinsPublishers*

Fount Paperbacks is an Imprint of
HarperCollins*Religious*
Part of HarperCollins*Publishers*
77–85 Fulham Palace Road, London W6 8JB

First published in Great Britain
in 1993 by Fount Paperbacks

3 5 7 9 10 8 6 4 2

A catalogue record for this book is
available from the British Library

ISBN 0 00 627633 4

Phototypeset by Intype, London
Printed and bound in Great Britain by
HarperCollinsManufacturing, Glasgow

# CONTENTS

# FOREWORD

It's my privilege.

Hold on. Privilege? Yes, that too. But rather it's my sheer, unbridled pleasure to occupy the editor's chair of a quite remarkable magazine.

Yes, yes, I would say that. But I say it, I believe, from a rather different perspective than most editors would adopt. What makes Saga magazine remarkable comes less from what's in it – though that's pretty good – and more from who reads it.

It has a personality, a warmth, a sort of communal spirit and drive that emanates largely from the stimulating people who read it, subscribe to it, write to it and influence it.

They – if you don't already know – are the retired. People who've ended full-time work to embark upon a new and fulfilling period in their lives. People who think, who reflect, who still yearn to learn, who look forward as much as they look back, whose collective wisdom and experience is perhaps the most undervalued asset this country possesses.

Until a couple of years ago, Saga magazine, I felt, was not complete. It lacked something. A simple, uplifting, spiritual message, perhaps one that would make anyone chancing upon it feel better for the encounter.

At first, a couple of clergymen strove valiantly to interpret my imprecise brief. Their offerings were long on theology, short on humanity. Where was the personal faith, the common touch, the searing light of simple belief that, I'd hoped, would inspire others?

Actually, it was out there all the time, in the hearts and minds of many of the two million readers who enjoy Saga magazine. It took a reader's letter to tap into it.

I must tell you a little about our readers' letters. They arrive like homing pigeons released from towns and villages all over the country, enormous flocks of them zooming unerringly in after delivery of every issue, to tell me what readers are thinking, criticizing, demanding, seeking or opposing. They are brilliant – relevant, cogent, literate and perceptive. The pages on which they are printed are the very heart of Saga magazine.

This particular letter came from a Mrs Marjory Davys: "Would it be possible," she wrote in part, "for your magazine to include a small section, perhaps contributed by readers, dealing with religious questions, doubts, thoughts, arguments, experiences? I simply hunger to exchange ideas with other people, but mostly people are too busy, or don't care."

Saga magazine published the letter, adding an editor's footnote welcoming the idea and inviting readers to send in 250-word contributions on the theme "I Believe". The date was November 1990.

By the time we reached the new year it had become evident that my invitation to contribute was carrying perhaps more weight than an invitation to a royal garden party. Saga readers *did* want to write about matters of faith.

Those of strong, unwavering belief wanted to share their convictions with others, perhaps to help them along the same path.

Others, lacking that absolute certainty, found that putting down the words to position themselves on the

"I Believe" map was not only helpful but itself inducing of clearer, stronger faith.

Yet more wrote about personal experiences, strange tales some, with a vigour and clarity to create images in my mind that linger still.

While some, with the candour which is an endearing character trait of the elders of this land, wanted to explain why they believed in not believing, if you see what I mean.

As individual testimonies, they were pretty impressive. But it was when you read them together, as I did every month to select one – yes, just one – for publication, that you became aware of their collective strength and richness.

Space limited us to publishing one per issue. Lamenting that fact in a leading article, I suggested that a compilation of "I Believe" stories would make for a splendid book, and invited any interested publishers to get in touch.

The rest, as they say, is history. I've just re-read Saga readers' "articles of faith" in the form in which they appear in the following pages, and I have to say that I find them as stimulating, challenging, provocative and moving as I did at first encounter.

I hope they do the same for you.

*Paul Bach*
*Editor, Saga magazine*

--------------------------------------------------------------------------

Saga magazine is available only by personal subscription. For details and a sample copy, please write to Saga magazine, FREEPOST, PO Box 60, Folkestone, Kent CT20 1AZ, and refer to Thora Hird's *I Believe* book.

# INTRODUCTION

You know those little stickers people put in the back window of their cars? They used to say "Running In – Please Pass" but today you get all sorts. You can usually guess from the kind of car what the message is likely to be. On the back of very small ones it'll be "My other car's a Rolls-Royce" and a rusty old boneshaker will bear the legend: "My wife's got the Ferrari"; on the wood-trimmed station wagons it's either "I ♥ Golden Retrievers" or "Keep Back! Baby on Board!"; a green Volkswagen will carry the message: "Save the Whale!" And my friend, Elizabeth Gort, who works with me on *Praise Be!*, and has helped me compile and edit the letters for this book, drives a Suzuki jeep with "I ♥ bell-ringing", which tells you that she's someone who enjoys ringing the church bells on Sunday mornings.

Well, I saw a new one the other day, which was obviously heartfelt, and would suit all of us *Saga* readers down to the ground. In the back window of a tidy little mini that was bowling along, an old man with flowing white hair and a beard at the wheel, I read:

"Old Age Ain't for Sissies!"

What a thought! But isn't it just so true? You learn a thing or two about bearing pain as you grow older. And about saying goodbye.

Not that I'm complaining. I've been very blessed, and in so many ways I don't feel any different now from when I was – well, all right, not twenty, perhaps – forty. Half my lifetime ago. Oh dear! I know I was born in May 1911, three years before the Great War started, and there's nothing wrong with my head for figures, but it still comes as a great surprise to me to realize that Scotty and I are now in our eighties . . .

There's one thing that I thank the Lord every day for: I'm still working. It's not just the nice feeling that people still want you – it's the fact that I still *can* work that I'm so grateful for. I'm sure that everyone who reads *Saga* knows that the secret of feeling young is to keep as busy and as interested in life as you can. I've even got a little card in my bedroom, that a fan kindly sent me, that says:

> YOU DON'T STOP DOING THINGS
> BECAUSE YOU GROW OLD –
> YOU GROW OLD
> BECAUSE YOU STOP DOING THINGS

I read it every day as I get up. But not everyone is lucky enough to be able to keep on working. For any actor or actress it's a great privilege to know that people still have faith in you and have work for you to do when you get to my age – and the more they ask me to do, the younger I feel!

Don't younger people have some funny ideas about us senior citizens? Have you ever noticed how someone can be a captain of industry one day, with secretaries and all sorts scurrying around to do his or her bidding, but from the day they retire, whenever people see them doing the shopping, or ordering a pint in the local, or hopping on a bus, they'll put on a sentimental voice and say, "Doesn't he do well?!" (As if they expect anyone who is retired to be in their dotage or daft!)

Now I mentioned the Great War just now. I suppose as far as children are concerned, I might just as well have written, "I was born at the time of the Norman Conquest" or "just before the Battle of Trafalgar". They may have "done it in history" but they can't revisit it in their memories – that other time, that other England, that we grew up in.

That's why Scotty and I enjoy reading *Saga* so much. The articles are mostly by or about people who have lived through the same little bit of history that we have, and it's like linking up with an extended family. Sometimes other people's reminiscences will bring to mind people and places *we* knew, or some old customs and sayings that had slipped away into the back of our minds, and it's lovely to be reminded of them.

Not that *Saga* is just about nostalgia. We're all still alive and kicking, praise the Lord, and life is for living. That's one reason why I especially like the Letters page, with its exchange of stories, views and ideas about everything under the sun – from deafness to bank charges, from milk puddings to the Gulf War.

I've also discovered that so many of you share our family's love of the natural world – which I think is something you come to appreciate more and more as you get older, don't you?

To give you a for instance, amongst the letters in the July 1992 issue, which I've just been reading (which I always do the minute the magazine arrives, if we're at home), was one about some mallards being, I suppose you could call it "shipwrecked without a ship". Now this interested me very much, because one of the great joys of recent years has been the arrival of some new neighbours at our home in the country: a family of mallards.

You might know that Scotty and I luckily and lovingly occupy a cottage in the grounds of our daughter Jan and her husband William's home, in a very beautiful part of rural East Sussex. Well, about four years ago Jan requested that if we were passing the tack room, would we please do so quietly, as she had noticed a mallard duck busily building a nest in the herbacious border opposite.

It was making a comfortable home, on the ground under a clematis that covered an old stone wall and fell over the border like a beautiful floral umbrella. The nest was entirely out of sight, and quite safe. However, the request to "please do everything quietly" was willingly obeyed.

As I'm sure you know, anything one does in a garden tack room always has a bit of noise to it . . . buckets, spades, forks, wheelbarrows all make a "bit of noise", however carefully you move them or pick them up. Scotty and I and Jan's gardener had to be seen to be believed all that summer, approaching the tack room on tiptoe, creeping in and out, carrying a bucket as though it was a Ming vase!

Nine beautiful eggs were laid, and the mallard was a devoted mother. She would fly off the nest each evening, out over the lake, and shortly afterwards return and settle back lovingly on her as yet unborn, shell-wrapped babies. The ducklings eventually cracked their shells and made their entrance into the floral world that surrounded them.

One day Mother Mallard, who knew Jan and William's grounds almost as well as they did themselves, took her babies for a special treat and waddled them all off to the heated swimming pool; Mother jumped in and her family all flopped in after her. Jan was passing the pool and saw the happy sight.

A little while later, as Jan passed the pool again, on her way back from feeding the hens, she saw Mother Mallard standing on the path, ordering her family to get out. Oh dear! They *couldn't* get out – the side of the pool was too steep! Mother Mallard was getting agitated and whatever it was she was saying in duck language, she was shouting it!

Jan ran to the shed nearby and collected some slats of wood in record time (one almost hears the "Dick Barton, Special Agent" music!) and rushed back to the scene of anguish (on Mother Mallard's part – the ducklings were still gaily bobbing about in the warm water). Mother even jumped in and out of the pool a few times, telling the babies to "do this!" Jan placed the slats of wood in the water, providing gangplanks for the little ones, and called out, "Anyone else going ashore?"

As soon as one brave duckling ran up the plank, the rest followed. Mother Mallard marched the little procession home, unmistakably quacking all the way, ". . . and that's the last time I take you anywhere!"

If you are as "soppy" or "daft" a family as we are, which I know many of you are, you will understand that the Mallard Family were now part of *our* family. The following year Mrs Mallard built her nest in exactly the same place. We were delighted, and once again we crept in and out of the tack room picking up our gardening implements as though we were stealing.

The only thing she hasn't been able to protect her young from has been the murderous minks, freed a few miles up the river by some "animal lovers" who objected to minks being caged. No duckling or chick was safe. Minks don't only kill to eat or feed their young, but also for the sheer joy of destroying – or that's what it seems like. Each morning there were more little heads lying apart from their poor mutilated bodies. Carnage. Do you wonder that whenever Jan and William's molecatcher gets a mink, you can hear our cheers a few miles up the river?

The following year we all waited to welcome Mrs Mallard back, but . . . no. We didn't see her about. We were sad, but we understood. Then one afternoon Jan was clipping dead heads off a large rose tree outside the dining room. Next to the rose tree was another clematis, and there, underneath the tent-like foliage, was Mother Mallard herself, and eleven babies! Scotty and I were having dinner over at Jan and William's that evening, and, believe me, the entire occasion was as exciting as when the Prodigal Son returned home, in the Bible story!

Last spring, 1992, Jan was looking out of the kitchen window, and there, waddling about the garden, were Mrs Mallard and her husband – looking just like any young married couple "viewing property"! (I don't mean that young married couples waddle. . . .) A few weeks later I remarked that I wondered where she had chosen to build her nest this year. "Oh!" said Jan, "I meant to tell you . . . come outside a minute." So out I went. Their gardens are a mass of blooms and scents, and in one corner, tucked under a beautiful rosemary bush which was a solid mass of flowers, was . . . yes . . . Mother Mallard and her family. I couldn't count how many because the ground was so covered in blooms. Clever girl! Welcome home!

I know you'll all understand why I get so much pleasure from that little part of our lives, because it's the sort of thing you write about, too, and why the Letters page of *Saga* is such a delight.

Another thing everybody is probably inclined to think about more as they get older is faith, and in particular what you believe about the afterlife. When more of your friends are with the Lord than are still here sharing the joys and woes of this life, well, you do just wonder, don't you? So I'm not surprised that when *Saga* editor, Paul Bach, decided to invite contributions for a 250-word "I believe" column, he ran into the same problem that I have to face every year on my television series, *Praise Be!*: too much choice!

I find it so hard to choose which ones to read out on the air, and only wish I could include more than just a tiny fraction of the wonderful letters I receive; now Paul Bach, too, has had hundreds of inspiring "I believe" contributions, but only the space to include one per issue.

And he has come up with the same solution that I did – a book! For the last two years I have been writing my *Praise Be!* books as a loving "thank you" to viewers, and in order to include more of the contributions I've received than can be fitted in "on air". So I was very glad, and honoured I might say, when *Saga* asked me to introduce this book – a collection of the very best "I believe" contributions that *Saga* readers have been sending in over the past two years, which all deserved to be published, but couldn't be because of the limited space of the magazine.

As the original idea of the column was to be an ideas "exchange", we've grouped the letters into themes, so that different sides to a question can be read one after the other. These letters, each and every one of them, are the result of the accumulated wisdom of a lifetime's experience, so you might know they are very thought-provoking. You won't agree with what everyone has written, but that's half the fun!

It's been a pleasure to read them all, and add a few thoughts to link them together. And, yes, I have even managed to write an ''I believe'' of my own – but you'll have to read the whole book to find that!

There's so much wisdom here, and humour, and love, I know you'll find it an inspiration. Thank you, fellow *Saga* readers, for letting me share the pleasure with you.

*Thora Hird*
*August 1992*

# PART ONE

## *All the World's a Stage*

I owe a great deal to writers, and have learnt so much from them in my life as an actress. Using their clever words I can show an audience the sadness and pain behind a character you also want to laugh at. What I especially like to play are what I call "ordinary" women – the sort of people who everyone knows but are inclined to underestimate or overlook – and showing the wisdom that these "ordinary" people have acquired in lifetimes which may look mundane, but deep down may be surprisingly joyful, or profoundly sad.

One of the greatest compliments I've ever received was paid to me only recently. It was on a radio programme about Alan Bennett, that wonderful writer whose observant, funny-sad plays I am always highly delighted to take part in. On the programme someone said. "Thora Hird is an actress who, like Alan Bennett with his writing, can make you laugh and cry in the same speech". I'm sure you understand why I feel that no one could say anything nicer.

These days I still get a lot of scripts sent to me, but the ones I choose to do are not necessarily the ones with big parts in them for me. What I look for are lines that I know I can do something with. I don't mind if I've only *one* line in the whole play, just so long as there's something in that line that will help me make that character "reach out and touch" the audience – with laughter or tears – and preferably a bit of both!

Reading through these "I believe" pieces that *Saga*

readers have written, although they are all about 250
words long (because that was what was called for), very
often it's just one sentence that stays in my mind, and
tells me all I would need to know about the letter writer
if I was asked to "play" them.

Jaques says in his famous speech in Shakespeare's *As
You Like It*, "one man in his time plays many parts", so
this first group of letters is mainly about the different
ages and stages of our lives, and the different moments
when we come to learn about God – to believe in Him
or *not* to believe, because, oh yes, *Saga* received plenty
of letters from agnostics, atheists and humanists, and
their views are down here, too.

Some of you have written that you believe that however old we grow, we will always have something to
learn – from children.

"At first the infant . . ."

**I believe . . .**
you must become as a little child

FROM MRS ELSPETH A. WALKER                    *Perth, Scotland*
                                              *12 December 1990*

My granddaughter Emma sings "Jesus loves me. This I know, for the Bible tells me so." Emma is nearly four. She has no problems with this belief. Childlike, but never childish, we too can have complete confidence in God's love for us.

I believe that we are born into this world with a deep desire to be with God, to know Him; to have a relationship with Him, but we have to learn, we have to be well taught, and we have to want to be like Jesus, to be with Him.

Being with God is not a reward for good deeds done on earth. Heaven is not something we "work" for. Being with God is his gift of grace given to us simply because we ask for it, and receiving it, we do what we can, to do His work, in His name.

However, the world keeps pulling us away from the way our Father wants us to go. Its values, ideals, standards and reasoning confuse and distract us. Even when we do know where we are going, loved ones and friends do not always understand that meeting and loving Jesus changes our world views. But it surely does.

As our relationship with our Lord deepens, the world

becomes more of an "alien" place to us, in the sense that we feel more strongly that we are passing through on our way to God.

I believe that our stay here is part of our eternal life, and as followers of Jesus, He is with us now, and we will be with him for ever.

Being with God always, I believe, *is* Heaven, here and now, as well as in the future.

I was well over fifty (having been a Christian for as long as I could remember) before I really began to understand what little Emma sings about.

**FROM MRS I. F. BROMWICH**          *Bognor Regis, Sussex*
                                        *26 April 1991*

I believe, indeed I KNOW, that the Lord gives us courage. A few months ago, my daughter, who teaches R.E. in a girls' school, said to her 11-year-olds, "For your 'prep' I want you to make a bookmark, decorate it and write on it a short text which would be of comfort to someone who was ill, or worried, or fearful."

One girl painted tiny pansies and leaves on hers, with the words,

The Lord is with me. I will not be afraid.

She presented it as a gift to her teacher, who said, "May I give it to my mother? She is not very well, and she would love it." The child readily agreed, and so I received the pretty bookmark at a time of serious illness when I was rather frightened.

The Creed begins, "I believe in God", but goes on to speak of Jesus Christ crucified, followed by the words, "He descended into hell." Sometimes we do, too. It is then that we need comfort, reassurance and uplift.

I did a lot of reading during that time of sickness, and I looked at my bookmark constantly. It certainly helped me to conquer my fear and has become one of my most treasured possessions.

It could be a real ministry for youngsters to make bookmarks like this, and give them to old or worried or sick people, a constant reminder that God cares, and will give them the courage they need.

He will also bring us confidence and courage at the hour of our dying. "It is I", he will whisper, "Be not afraid."

FROM MRS V. C. JOHNSON *Prestbury, Cheshire*
*10 November 1990*

The advantage of being old is the ability to speak from experience. I truly believe that when I was four I knew God. It was natural to talk to Him. When I grew older I realized how presumptuous I was. Yet did not Christ say: "Suffer the little children to come unto me"?

I had Scripture at day school and attended Sunday School. I enjoyed the parables. Maybe my views were being conditioned unconsciously, but, they were quite apart from the ones I had of God.

Now I am eighty and still need to open my heart to Him. Now I also listen to His voice. He speaks through the Bible and His words have to be digested slowly. Understanding brings joy.

Does one truly mean all one says when repeating the Lord's Prayer? "Forgive us our trespasses as we forgive them that trespass against us . . ." Not always easy. To try is the only way to progress spiritually.

It took me a long time to learn that God loves us in

spite of our faults, and we must try to do the same with others, even when human nature does not want to be tolerant.

When I look into the eyes of a trusting child, I feel the child is looking back with the eyes of God. Then I know His world will continue, regardless of evil. It is our duty to give thanks for all that makes our lives and His world beautiful.

FROM MRS STELLA TASSELL                    *Woking, Surrey*

I wish my church was more like my grandchildren.

Matthew is a tough and burly rugby player, enjoying the rough and tumble of life. He recognizes academic subjects as necessary but boring details which hold school life together and so enable him to get on with the REAL things – football, cricket, baseball, etc.

Katie is the academic. Although she enjoys lots of activities such as Guides, dancing and swimming, the REAL things for her are history, maths and science.

Anna is a dreamer. She enjoys school, but would rather be at home writing stories and imagining situations and happenings far beyond the ideas of most eleven-year-olds.

Their house is always full of other children and adults.

My church is a little bit like the grandchildren.

Some of us like the rough and tumble of REAL Christianity; youth work, evangelism, rousing choruses, movement and change within the worship.

Others are more interested in keeping the teaching and theological standards clear and true. These are the REALITIES of church life.

Some of us are dreamers, visionaries, contemplatives.

The REAL world consists more of thoughts and prayer than of physical activity or group projects.

The difference between my church and my grand-children seems to be in the ability to love and accept each other as we are.

The children tease, argue and laugh at each others' strange ways, but they don't try to change each other. They have learnt from their parents that each of them is precious just as he or she is.

At church each group seems to be trying to change the others. To help the others to see the Realities of Christianity in the same way as themselves. So there are tensions, misunderstandings, and hurt pride.

We are not accepting and loving each other just as we are: creatures very precious to God.

Maybe this is why people do not crowd into our church as they do into the grandchildren's house.

<br>

**FROM MARY SCOPES** *Woodbridge, Suffolk*
*31 May 1991*

Come with me, if you will, along my memory lane. As an infant teacher, I gained much experience in different schools. However, one special occasion I treasure very much. It was in a village school.

Each morning we would chat for a few minutes about the lovely world of nature around us, things to look for in the fields, hedgerows and woods. In March 1970 we talked especially about our favourite wild flowers which would soon be in bloom. My favourite wild flower is a dandelion.

One morning, weeks later, my children greeted me with the words "You cannot go into our classroom until we call you." Obviously something was afoot. The moment arrived. I was asked to "Come in."

Breathtaking!! My table was covered with dandelion flowers in full bloom – all tightly packed. The children must have cleared the entire village of dandelions.

Smiling faces eagerly awaited my reaction. Frankly I was very near to tears – those dear little children had known me for less than a term, yet remembered I loved dandelions. How quietly each child stood.

I thanked them, saying the beautiful yellow flowers were "like a cushion of sunshine".

At the back of the room, standing on a chair, so as to view the proceedings, was a little boy not quite five years old. In broad Suffolk dialect he called out: "Thass God's sunshine, in't it, Miss?"

That morning indeed a little child told us all how to believe.

**FROM JOHN BROWN**                    *Marazion, Cornwall*
                                       *13 February 1991*

As I get older I realize how much more resistant to change I am becoming. I do things as I have always done. I think as I have always done. It works for me. I avoid making mistakes and life goes on comfortably, and without the traumas of earlier days.

But I realize that in the last 100 years there has been more change in the world than in the whole history of mankind since Ur was founded way back in antiquity. There are more people out there now doing greater things than were ever done in the past. Modern counterparts of Shakespeare, Einstein, Beethoven, Galileo, St Francis and St Paul, are all out there right now, not to be recognized or discovered until long after I have departed. But I must not be unaware of their presence, and I should try to listen to the collective wisdom of present ages. I must not close my mind to change and I must try, even though it will be hard, to learn to recognize that as a planet we are now travelling in the fast lane, and adjust my driving attitudes accordingly.

This does not mean challenging the God-given truths as propounded by Jesus and the great prophets, but only some of the interpretations that past societies have found it expedient to place upon them.

I think about our traditional respect for property, and the young people's protest via vandalism and graffiti. I think of our great concern about keeping up appearances, and the young people's protest via faded jeans and weird hair-dos. I think of the mixed marriages or non-marriages. Of the music that seems to depend totally upon shouting and banging something.

At the beginning of the last century there were only about 8 million people in the British Isles. When Jesus lived there were probably fewer than 8 million in the whole world. As a society we have been successful. So successful that we now have 60 million of us in the British Isles alone, and over five billion worldwide.

I ask myself, are we still, here and now, on our way out of the Garden of Eden? The whales, seals, elephants and tigers might think so.

Are we still worshipping the golden calf? A look at the pollution levels might give us food for thought.

I believe, for all their raucous clumsiness, there is a collective message coming from the young people of today. I believe we should listen and try to understand what they are trying to say.

I believe, even though we find it disturbing and uncomfortable, that we should be prepared for change.

FROM BETTY MORRIS                    (*in* Saga, *March 1991*)

A few years ago we had in our parish a priest who was much loved by everyone in the area, whether church-goers or not. Sadly he is now dead.

One day a mother who was collecting her little boy from playgroup in the church hall said to him, "Look! There's Father Murphy."

"That's not Father Murphy," said the child. "That's God."

I have often thought how truly that little child spoke. Many of us are like Philip, who asked Jesus to let him see the Father, not recognizing God with a human face.

Although Jesus is one with the Father in a special sense, because he is true God and true Man, he told his followers, "I am in my Father and you are in me and I in you."

When God seems far away, it is comforting to realize that he is in those we love and in those who love us – and in us too, however much we may soil his image.

In a world in which many are lonely and long for some kind of faith, we need to recall that little boy's words and recognize that God has a human face.

"Unwillingly to school . . ."

**I believe . . .**
we must teach our children about
God

FROM MRS W. WADE

*Clapham, London*
*8 November 1990*

The dusty, grey, wooden stairs wound upwards to the odd-shaped corner room from which streamed light.

Sunday School with the welcoming smile of the Vicar's daughter. How many times had Jane and I climbed those dim-lit stairs? More than a hundred in the end, with a Bible so inscribed.

The teacher held us quiet and attentive, her faith shining through her long forgotten words, kindling a tiny flame in young, thoughtless hearts. The favourite choruses are with me still. They reflect those lost words that started feet walking a path to confirmation – I believe.

I did, but the step of faith has to be taken constantly. Prayers offered, answered, refused, but still the belief goes on, through dark valleys to sunlit heights of praise.

A journey started all those years ago, leading to a trust in the One who is with us always, even to the end.

"Lord, I believe. Help Thou mine unbelief."

FROM MRS KAY SHORE                *Halifax, West Yorkshire*

My belief is fundamental to me. I grew up with it; it's part of me and I've never felt the need to doubt or question it. God is just THERE, watching over us, ready to help us over the bumpier bits of life.

An early childhood memory is the bedtime prayer I was taught – the first verse of Gentle Jesus – which my mother used to say for me until I could recite it for myself. (And what a mouthful that line "Pity my simplicity", is, for a tiny child to enunciate!)

In those days life was centred around church activities. Chapel and Sunday School on Sundays; Girls' Brigade and Young People's Fellowship during the week. The annual events like Sales of Work, Boys' Brigade Parents and Friends Night, Harvest Festival and its Fruit Banquet, the Christmas Nativity Play. And, for me, the supreme moment was baptism by immersion as a young adult – following Christ through the Waters of Baptism.

Perhaps faith was "indoctrinated" into me, but if that is so, I'm glad it was. Over the years it has helped me to cope with anxieties, and with the loss of loved ones. I cannot imagine how unbelievers can come to terms with bereavement. Death must seem so final if one has no hope that there is anything to follow. I am not yet ready to find out for myself what there is beyond the grave, but I thank God for my belief that He has some plan.

FROM MR SYDNEY HETHERINGTON
C. ENG., M. I. MECH. E                *Eastbourne, Sussex*
                                        *6 November 1990*

May I put the case for the non-believer, the agnostic?

I began my life as a Christian. My parents, following

the expectations of the neighbours, had me christened, I attended Sunday School and took Religious Instruction at my day schools. My own children were christened, not because we, as parents, believed, but because it was expected of us. I made no secret of the fact that I was not a believer. At the same time I did not, and do not, attempt to persuade others to share my disbelief.

By what right then do the "believers", whether they be Christian, Muslim, Buddhist or whatever, tell me how to conduct my life? I do my bit for the less fortunate, I have a social conscience, I don't attack or rob my neighbour. If I was a small shopkeeper, why should I take Sunday off? Why not Monday when trade is slack? Why should I not be able to go and buy a book (even a Bible) on a Sunday?

Yes, I do believe. I believe in freedom, freedom from religious intolerance, freedom to do what I wish, providing that it does no harm to my neighbour. The freedom, indeed, for which wars have been fought.

FROM MRS ELSIE K. CROSS　　　　*Bury St Edmunds, Suffolk*

To write about "Why I believe in God" gave me quite a task, for I can't remember a time when I haven't believed.

It isn't as if I was brought up to believe. I can never remember God being mentioned to me by my mother or father, although they were strict, in so far as we didn't play ball on Sundays, but no reason given why.

I never met my grandparents, though I do know my paternal grandfather was a much respected Salvation Army Officer. I have a newspaper cutting of his funeral, and much was said of his great faith and service for the Lord. He was 45 years old when he died. (Could it be that his prayers were answered, in that three of us sisters were brought to know the Lord personally?) Apparently after his first wife died he married again, and my father as a young lad suffered much under his stepmother, which may have caused him loss of faith.

At twelve years of age, I was converted through the Open Air Mission, but became a wanderer (prodigal) but I never lost my faith, neither did God let me go.

I was brought back through the Faith Mission in 1951. My faith was assured and more personal. Wonderful answers to prayer have confirmed my faith.

The feeling of warmth within, assuring me of the Lord's presence in my life, has been, and is, very powerful at times.

Where do people turn for comfort and peace of heart and mind if they have no belief?

Part of a song that the Bachelors used to sing comes to mind, and I quote:

I believe above the storm, the smallest prayer
Will still be heard.
I believe that someone in the great somewhere
Hears every word.
Every time I hear a newborn baby cry,
Or touch a leaf
Or see the sky
Then I know why
I believe.

FROM MRS MURIEL PEARS                  *Keswick, Cumbria*
                                            *1 May 1991*

I believe that *Saga* people should start a SOCIETY for the SLOWING DOWN and PRESERVATION of CHILDHOOD (SSPOCH). Instead of a subscription, members would invest their time, skills, attention and imagination.

Children with a SSPOCH friend would find that having someone to share their play can be better than being bought things. An evolving, make-believe game of Schools or Houses (though the little boy I know best prefers Plumbers, Burglars or Being Santa Claus on Christmas Eve), played with an adult whose certain rule for all such games is a genuine willingness to join in, brings a contentedness that a new toy rarely does.

There is a pace for reading a book with children. Outsiders might go too fast. SSPOCH people would know that bits need to be savoured, perhaps re-read, that pictures need to be studied, and, at the end, recollections of special incidents need to be contemplatively shared.

SSPOCH would be against bikinis at four and school satchels at five, over-detailed or premature sex education, the piercing of tiny ears, and the bombardment of young children with news of war and disaster. Children have enough fears of their own.

Members would be for summer play in parks and gardens, board and card games in winter, and the exposing of children to the cycle of seasons. They would stop to look, with children, at raindrops on webs, snails' trails and daffodils about to open, and listen, with positive and responsive interest, to a child's intricate descriptions of his makings and doings.

Members would take grandchildren or young friends on safe street walks, where gardens, manholes, door knockers, house names, wrought iron gates and traffic signs offer free opportunities for shared study of beauty, design and utility.

There are bonuses for members. They are the sessions of personal relaxations which come from joining children walking and looking, at their pace, and being welcomed into their world – playing, in fact.

Wordsworth, in his famous Ode, wrote, "Heaven lies about us in our infancy." It needs to. Life sends too many brickbats later. So, wear the invisible SSPOCH badge, and ensure that each small child of your acquaintance enjoys his share of slow-motion heaven.

**FROM MRS MURIEL ANDERSON** *Edinburgh*
*5 October 1990*

As a child, a feeling of security came to me from the verse:

> Jesus loves me, He who died
> Heaven's Gate to open wide,
> He will wash away my sin,
> Let His little child come in.

My much loved grandmother wished to share her joyous faith. Shy about speaking it, she wrote in 1870, and had printed, the following verses, which she would hand to people she met in railway carriages etc.

## The Love of Jesus

Anxious sinner, dost thou see
That earnest, yearning look to thee,
Given in love from Calvary's tree,
    By Jesus?

That pierced side and bleeding brow
Proclaim salvation even now.
Look and your soul shall humbly bow
    To Jesus.

Full atonement has been made,
God's demands have all been paid.
Thy many sins have all been laid
    On Jesus.

Trust then, and cast away your fears,
Your sins, self-righteousness and tears.
Rejoice, for boundless grace appears
    In Jesus

In 1875 she was widowed, with three little children, soon to become five, as my mother and her twin sister were born after their father's death. All five became committed Christians and married committed Christians.

I thus grew up, blessed by Christian influences, and have met many, in my long life, whose selfless lives, radiating Christ's love, made the presence of God's Spirit felt in a very real way.

I know God as my Father, Jesus as my Saviour and His Spirit, through daily reading of my Bible, as my Counsellor.

**FROM MRS PATRICIA OLIVER**                     *Fife, Scotland*
                                                  *24 January 1991*

For my part this letter should be "Do I believe?" because I am an absolute doubting Thomas.

I have attended church regularly, from Sunday School – where I was always in trouble for asking awkward questions – to being a member of the choir until I married and moved to Scotland.

All my life I've worked diligently for the Church – in the vestry, doing the altar linen and the gardens, etc. etc. Perhaps if I had kept aloof from the everyday running of things I would have found it easier to believe.

It's very difficult to keep faith and run a church function. Indeed, it's very hard to be a Christian *and* a working member of a church. There's an awful lot of pettiness and intolerance to contend with.

I have always shunned the popular discussion groups, where religion is studied "in depth". Too much depth would be the end of me.

But Christianity *has* stood the test of time, so there *must* be something in it. There is only one way that we will know if it is true, and that is when we die. Going to church is a bit like getting stamps on your insurance card.

One thing I am convinced about is that, if we all led our lives as Jesus taught, the world would be a much better place.

When I have problems, I say to myself, "What would Jesus have done?" and there is my answer. So maybe I do believe after all.

"then, a soldier . . ."

**I believe . . .**
you must hold on to what you know
is right

FROM JOHN MCFARLAN                                *Glasgow*
                                          (in Saga, *September 1991*)

I was still in my teens when I arrived at the recruitment centre in Glasgow to join the Army. A son of the manse, the storms of life had passed me by.

The Colour Sergeant, resplendent in his dress uniform of the Cameronians, was a huge man with a fierce, bristling moustache and a row of medals which stretched across his broad chest. I trembled inwardly when I saw him.

My medical being over, I took the Oath and he gave me the King's shilling. I was now a soldier. I waited to be dismissed.

"Listen, son," he said gently, "you will meet many enemies out there in the world, and they won't all be Germans. You will have temptations and hazards to overcome. Stick to your principles and your upbringing, and you will win through. Good luck, son."

Fifty years on I try to follow the old Colour Sergeant's good advice. I shall never forget him and the kind words of encouragement he gave me.

FROM MRS B. MARROW    *Lowton, near Warrington, Lancashire*
*27 October 1990*

## *I would like to Truly Believe*

My mother, despite a tragic bereavement, had an unshakeable faith, which she tried to instil in me by example, never force.

From early childhood I attended Sunday School; then church, becoming a Junior Churchwarden until joining the Army at age eighteen. Within weeks circumstances made me proclaim my faith at a Padre's meeting we were compelled to attend. The Padre closed the meeting by dismissing everyone except me. He then told me that as I spoke, he had a vision that God was calling me into His service, and quickly persuaded me to enrol as a Service Ordinand. For the remainder of my stay at the camp he encouraged and guided me into believing that that was my destiny.

But at the next camp the Padre was positively hostile, and at a subsequent, very large camp, there were two padres, elderly, pleasantly benign, but completely apathetic as far as my future was concerned.

My contemporaries respected me, but "old sweats" deliberately sought me out to challenge my beliefs, and though I defended them, I knew they were weakening and being replaced with doubts. So eventually I resigned.

Forty-five years later, despite having read the Bible from cover to cover, those doubts still remain.

There are more people alive today than have lived ever since the world began. The majority of them do not believe in God, or at least a Christian God. If heaven is only reserved for "true believers" then the other place is going to be extremely overcrowded. But how many "true believers" do, as Christ commanded, "To enter heaven, give *all*, and follow me."?

Oh for my mother's unshakeable faith!

FROM MRS J. R. THORPE                    *Haywards Heath, Sussex*

As the Bible instructs us, I believe the most important thing of all is belief itself! At the end of the day, the truth of the words "All things are possible to him that believeth" will prove their validity. That is, if you really believe it, of course!

It is imperative to accept that it is one's own beliefs which matter, and not anyone else's. We should never be deflected by another person's doubts or ridicule; it is their loss! If it works for us, that is not only all that matters, but is in itself the key.

As the years pass we have time to review the jigsaw of our lives. Now we see that the bad things were precursors of greater and happier events to come. We needed to go through the tunnels to prepare us for the dazzling sunshine beyond.

Devastating redundancy freed me to begin a new chapter from which grew hitherto unimagined benefits. A car accident gave unexpected time to take up a new hobby which in turn led to a whole new world of friendship and adventure.

My predominant and enduring Christian belief, proved to my delighted satisfaction on countless occasions, is that good invariably comes out of what is temporarily masquerading as evil. I now almost welcome the bad things and look expectantly over their shoulder for the excitements to come! And they always do!

**FROM MR W. H. BROOMFIELD**           *Lymington, Hampshire*

There is no better time than old age to reach a conclusion about the nature of religion. One then has the
advantage of evidence, accrued from a lifetime of
experience, in my own case 77 years.

My first contact with the real world and doubts about
Christianity was on joining the British Army at 14 years
of age. A venture which I approached fearlessly, under
the influence of the heavy religious indoctrination,
common to childhood at that time. Seen in retrospect,
my naivety was breathtaking. There was the absurdity
of such sayings as "Blessed are the meek, for they shall
inherit the earth" and "Blessed are the pure in heart",
which had no relevance in the Army. There was the
incompatibility of the soldier's role with the fifth com-
mandment.

Doubts and uncertainty increased with the return to
civil life and with old age. Finally in retirement and
reflecting on the evidence, the scales, as they say, fell
from my eyes, with the realization that religion and
Christianity in particular, was a fantasy. Whereupon all
the facts of the matter fell into place, like the resolution
of a Miss Marple murder mystery.

With this revelation, the doubts and mysteries dis-
solved, among which was that of my failure, over a
long, adventurous lifetime, never to have seen an
Angel, or a miracle, or a statue move, or to have known
even one person who had been struck down for telling
a lie.

FROM MRS DOROTHY HOLDEN                              *Preston, Lancashire*

I believe that without some central belief or force in life, the whole purpose of living would become a vacuum which at the first sign of stress, whether it be anxiety – so often purposeless – or other form of strain, our lives would be made unnecessarily unhappy.

Our original belief or trust in life must come from one's parentage – and how fortunate if we were brought up by Christian parents who by their everyday lives and firm beliefs taught us to trust and live by good ways.

Greatly to be pitied, in my opinion, are those who profess no belief in anything, often saying they don't need any sustenance apart from themselves and their own ability to earn sufficient money to purchase a kind of security based on worldly success.

A true belief will carry a person through tremendous strains – as witness the heroism of many men and women in time of war, who came through great suffering and tragedy and yet remained believers.

Many people turn to God during illness and great sorrow – and find Him always there as a sustaining power, and if we follow that Leader, He will help us to a belief that the inevitable Eternity is not to be feared, but will bring us to a Light more powerful than anything man can offer or devise – and it is there for each one of us as we say "I believe" – I prove it every day.

FROM AUGUSTA BEVIN          *Market Harborough, Leicestershire*
                                        *13 November 1990*

I was brought up C. of E. and was confirmed at 14, having learnt the Creed etc. to recite parrot-fashion. It wasn't until I was 16 and learnt from Roman history lessons what odd things the people were taught to believe in, that I realized I had been brainwashed. I still cherished parts of the New Testament, but explored other avenues for something my logical mind could believe in.

Now, at the age of 79, I can write of my conclusions.

I consider the most misleading statement in the Bible is: "And God made man in his own image". The great creative force which church people refer to as "Almighty and everlasting God, maker of Heaven and earth" (not to mention the rest of the universe) bears no relation to man, however glorified. To me this is not "He" but "It". The people Hiawatha belonged to had a better name for it – the Great Spirit.

Man, at his present stage of evolution, cannot comprehend infinity nor, I believe, the nature of the creator of the universe.

So he must be guided by wise men and prophets of all ages, such as Jesus of Nazareth and Mohammed, while he is earthbound, and so far as the rest of his life is concerned, he would do well to say with the Agnostic: "I DO NOT KNOW."

FROM MRS J. A. FRENZEL                    *Ipswich, Suffolk*
                                        *(in Saga, February 1991)*

I believe God IS, and that he is a tremendous power for good in the world.

I was fortunate enough to have been taught the difference between right and wrong from the start, and to say prayers and hear about Jesus at Sunday School. So I can't remember a time when I didn't know that good was for Jesus and that Jesus (who became God after my childhood) was the only power beyond mortal ones upon whom we could rely. The older I got, the more I realized the limitations of mortal powers – my own or anyone else's.

It has taken long years – sometimes of plain sailing, of great happiness, of believing, of not believing, of sitting on the fence – for me to come back to a steady, simple belief in God.

I no longer need to ponder, argue about, or find an explanation for the immaculate conception, the appearance of angels, or any of the other mystical events surrounding my belief. Many present-day phenomena and occurrences are mystery to me, and I accept that it is useless to try to understand by delving into them.

So I am happy and content to accept the great comfort and help in just simply believing and continuing to try to do the right thing to the best of my ability in order to get closer to my ultimate goal, which is peace and harmony within myself.

This, I believe, will help me to override the times of trial, tribulation and suffering which are an inevitable part of all our lives on earth.

"one man in his time plays many parts"

## I believe . . .
God has a purpose for each one of us

FROM MRS N. JOHNSON

*Clacton-on-Sea, Essex*
*20 December 1990*

I believe that God has a purpose for each one of us. Often it is hard to see what this might be; perhaps we are tied down with responsibilities, or are not well off, or are getting old. I discovered long ago that the best way to find out is to go to God himself, in prayer, and ask Him.

"Lord, what can I do for you? Use me in any way you can."

When I was tied to the house with young children and had very little money, I prayed this prayer, and the answer came to me that I could write letters. So I wrote to relations, friends, and anyone whom I knew was lonely or worried. I kept this up over many years, and I'm sure it helped cement friendships and certainly helped me.

All through my life I have prayed the "Use me" prayer. Through it I became involved with a mission in my church; with Lee Abbey, where my husband and I helped with the Summer Youth Camp for a number of years; with the Marriage Guidance Council; and then in my mid-forties I felt guided to become a late entrant to the teaching profession.

What can any of us do? Seemingly small things, often; maybe in our own church or neighbourhood, visiting, listening, offering a cup of tea to someone who is alone.

What God sends for you to do isn't always easy. But be very sure, if you ask God to use you, He will.

FROM MISS N. D. JONES *Liverpool, Merseyside*

I believe that God has a purpose for each one of our lives; if we follow His guidance, we can fulfil it.

I always wanted to be a teacher, from my early childhood. I never wavered from that desire.

I went through school and college; I got a post in an infant school; I enjoyed the work, but had no wish for promotion.

At the end of the Second World War, the Deputy Head decided to go on Exchange to America. As the teacher who came to us from Texas was strange to our ways, she was not asked to take on the post of responsibility. As next in seniority, I was asked to do it.

At the end of twelve months our Deputy came back, and took over her duties again. "Now you've done the job, why don't you apply for a Deputy's post?" she said.

I did, and got one quite soon.

I had only been at my new school a short time when the Head had to be absent for a long period to have an operation. I had to take charge of the school! Having had that experience, I decided to apply for a Headship. After some attempts, I got one.

I have had no desire for promotion, but I believe that that was God's plan for me!

FROM MRS PATRICIA DUCE          *St Leonards-on-Sea, East Sussex*
                                              *27 April 1991*

As I approach my allotted three-score-years-and-ten I believe more than ever that those who love God "have his aid and interest in everything", as it says in the Bible. And it makes sense that loving means obeying.

This promise had held good in many instances in my life, big and small, since deciding, many years ago, I would take seriously this important point of obedience to God's leading.

Almost immediately after deciding this, it so happened that my boss asked me to arrange for a French girl to come to England for a month's experience in our office, in the northern outskirts of London.

On the day of her planned arrival I was just setting off to go up to London to meet her train at Victoria Station, when the thought came to my mind to buy some flowers first, and leave them as a welcome at the digs I'd arranged for her. I rejected this, feeling I'd already done plenty in making all the arrangements. However, the thought persisted, so I somewhat grudgingly gave in.

The door was opened by an agitated landlady who was at that precise moment in the middle of taking a phone call from the Newhaven immigration authorities; they had detained the girl as she had no work permit. Taking over the telephone, I was able to explain to their satisfaction the special circumstances of her short-stay visit, and all was well.

If I hadn't called at that very moment, the girl would have been turned back to France, and I would have waited in vain at the station.

A vivid reminder of the importance of heeding the "inner voice".

FROM MRS KATHLEEN WHITE     *Swindon, Wiltshire*
*13 November 1990*

During my two and a half years as a WRNS photographer attached to the Fleet Air Arm, I met many different characters from all walks of life. While we were spending several hours a day developing and printing we had plenty of opportunities to chat to each other and in the kindly, anonymous darkness discussed quite frankly our backgrounds, families and hopes for the future whenever the war might end.

Bob, however, was special. He stood out from all the rest. A teenager like myself, he appeared to have everything going for him. Even the undistinguished uniform of an ordinary naval rating enhanced his slim figure. His brilliant eyes flashed as we exchanged jokes and comments. When he returned to the ship after a weekend in town, he talked about people and places of entertainment that I should never encounter.

His father had recently been appointed as a Professor at Oxford and the family home had become a lovely ancient stone building in the medieval side streets of the city.

Small wonder that I, the third child of a humble railway clerk, coming from a terrace house in a sooty suburb of a Yorkshire industrial city, envied him. The fairies seem to have given him all the good gifts at his christening I thought, with memories of the Sleeping Beauty's abundant fortune.

We were good friends, but all the same how I resented his almost unlimited assets compared with my meagre material resources!

Then one day, the tables were completely turned. We were chatting casually, when his face suddenly clouded and he spoke to me in deadly seriousness for once.

"How I envy you, Kathy, how I envy you! You've got your faith and I have simply none at all. I'd give everything I possess for that."

From that moment I humbly realized that I possessed the most precious thing that really mattered after all.

FROM MR BARRIE L. WILLIAMS          *Barry, South Glamorgan*
*1 November 1990*

Now at 76, I believe implicitly God loves, understands and, in His own good time, will reveal all. I can wait.

Meanwhile, following a busy life, I try to do what I can in a lesser but still practical way. I write some verse and many, many letters to friends, the papers or indeed anyone whom I think could do with a boost – or a word of thanks. Appreciative replies from Ministers of broadcast services alone confirm that this helps. And that "religion still matters" is in this sentence of the last delivered: "Amazingly, 282 letters have been received in response to our service."

Contact starts with you. Try it. Meanwhile, I pass on this prayer I wrote for myself.

> Fighting, falling, climbing, crawling,
> A battle all the way;
> Struggling, stumbling, loving, grumbling –
> This is, God, my day.

> Leading, pleading, worn and bleeding,
> Guide me, God, I pray;
> Laughing, weeping, waking, sleeping –
> Mould me in Thy way.

Choose me, use me, Dear God, prove me,
Forgive me when I stray;
Make me, break me, at last take me –
And bring me home some day.

# PART TWO

## *Friends and Neighbours*

I'm "on location"! And I've been sitting here in my room in a Huddersfield hotel, writing these little introductions by hand on the backs of some old scripts I've brought with me. I always re-use scripts that are sent to me – long before it became a vogue word I was "*recycling*" scripts, often for writing to Jan when she was living in America (I used to write her proper letters, too, of course, but we made sure that she got something *every day* to know that we were thinking about her – and sometimes it could only be a little loving note on the back of a script when I was rehearsing); and most of the stories in my memoirs *Scene and Hird* began life as little scribbles on the backs of scripts!

I'm "waiting in the wings" I suppose you might say, because I'm up here filming a new series of *The Last of the Summer Wine*. And whenever I'm not needed, I settle down to write another story.

I've been coming "up north" to film every summer for quite a few years now. Before I joined the cast of *The Last of the Summer Wine* there used to be *In Loving Memory* and *Allelujah!*, all filmed in this northern part of England where I grew up. I sometimes think I must be British Rail's best customer.

These weeks spent in the north are not quite the "homecoming" you might think – although I do get great pleasure when there's someone with a car and we've time to go out and about and visit some of the old market towns and beauty spots I remember from when I was young. But home is where the heart is, as they say, and although Morecambe and Lancashire will always be the setting of all my dearest memories of childhood, today "home" is with Scotty; and he's not here.

I am never really happy staying in a hotel on my own – although the management here have been kindness itself, and the cast and crew are all like one big family at the end of the day's work. There are still times of loneliness. That's part of an actor's life, which is perhaps not obvious to people who think it's all very glamorous. But a lot of time is spent when no one needs you, but you have to be there, waiting for when they do. I'm here to tell you, Scotty and home seem a long way away sometimes, and I dread to think what our telephone bill is going to be, but he's just as much to blame as I am!

I've never been someone who enjoys their own company, and during the times when I've not been needed "on the set" this year, I've been very glad to have something to occupy my mind and time. It's been like having company, having your *Saga* letters to think about! I know they weren't addressed to me personally, so they are not quite the same as the *Praise Be!* letters, which bring me so much pleasure in the early part of the year, but I have found myself agreeing with so much of what has been written (and then there are some letters with which I strongly *disagree*, so I'm sitting here nodding and smiling, and then violently shaking my head – it's a good job nobody is watching!), and it's been just like making a whole lot of new friends.

Friends have been such an important part of Scotty's and my life, and it's funny how many of our dearest friends are much younger than us – but they help us to keep feeling young.

This part of the book contains accounts about the ways *Saga* readers have found God through other people – through a friend, a neighbour, the family, through church, through prayers wonderfully – and sometimes surprisingly – answered, and through sudden conversion at huge gatherings, like Billy Graham's Missions.

In a word, nearly every one of this next group of letters seems to be saying:

"I believe that God is Love."

"People who need people are the
luckiest people . . .".

**I believe . . .**
God has a human face

**FROM BARBARA LAWSON**                    *Sussex*
*(in* Saga, *April 1991)*

I believe my mother had the secret of happiness. She
was always pleasant to people. I remember, in the
1930s, a short plump man with a black beard and a
black hat who used to come regularly along our road
of two-up-and-two-down terraced houses. We called
him the gramophone man.

My mother would say, "Oh, look at that poor man,"
as door after door was slammed in his face. Behind
lace curtains we watched him, sometimes dripping with
rain, approach our front door. My mother would welcome him into the best room, give him a cup of tea and
then say to us, "Now, sit still, children, and listen to
the gramophone."

There were five of us under the age of ten. We knew
the ritual and were usually already sitting, as good as
gold, in the upright chairs, the baby on my lap. We
then listened, for what seemed an eternity of time, to
the religious message on the gramophone. The words
seemed strange and gloomy. We were a little nervous
of "the gramophone man" but my mother used to say,
"Poor man. You never know what he has to put up
with."

For nearly three years he was the only man who sat in our front room, as my father was serving in submarines in China.

As the gramophone played, he sat like a statue, staring back at the wide-eyed children who watched him. I cannot remember him speaking. I think he was a Jehovah's Witness. He would raise his hat and smile at us as he left to continue on his way along the road.

None of us became a Jehovah's Witness. But we did learn a basic truth of goodness: kindness to other people.

**FROM MRS CONNIE HAZELL**      *Bournemouth, Dorset*

I believe that a sense of the ridiculous is one of the greatest gifts we can have bestowed upon us.

Everyone agrees that a sense of humour is essential if we are to survive the knocks and frustrations which life can mete out to us. We all know, too, how much easier it is to befriend a cheerful person, and how much better we feel for having met someone who greets us with a smile.

I believe, however, that a sense of the ridiculous is something more. It includes the ability to laugh at ourselves. It is the impishness left over from childhood, and it sees the comic side of a situation which would otherwise depress or dismay. It can have its disadvantages, of course, when we see humour on a serious occasion and it becomes our downfall, but I think it is worth the risk!

I recall an elderly, arthritic friend, about five feet nothing, being told by a hearty hospital nurse to "hop up on that table" indicating an examination table almost as high as the patient!

An aunt of mine, aged 89 and housebound, was visited by an earnest young man who, on leaving, told her to "exercise caution". She said she had visions of taking a dog called "Caution" out for a long walk!

Younger people do sometimes appear thoughtless in what they say. A sense of the ridiculous can stop us taking offence, and puts the whole thing into proportion.

Besides, it helps to keep us young!

**FROM MRS L. SHAH** *Enfield, Middlesex*

I believe that charity begins at home. We came to this country as refugees. We stayed at a friend's place for one month. At that time it was easy to find jobs. Me and my husband started working within one week of coming to this country. We did not think of social security – our first priority was to get jobs.

As soon as we started to work, we were able to move to one bedroom, shared bathroom, shared kitchen accommodation. In about two years' time we were able to put a deposit to buy our own house. As soon as we settled, our house has been a base for other members of our family.

I believe we should help "less well off" members of our own family before giving money to charities.

I am forever grateful to the friend who helped us by letting us stay at his house.

**FROM THE REV. SAM BALLANTYNE** *Aberdeen*

"Amazing grace, how sweet the sound
that saved a wretch like me."

The love of God has sustained me into the "borrowed years". As an ordained minister of the Church of Scotland for half a century, I count my blessings. It has been a great privilege to deal with so many kind and courageous people in the crucial experiences of illness, bereavement and suffering, as well as gladsome events such as baptism and marriage.

It must be difficult for folk with no spiritual foundation to deal with the traumatic experiences that come to all of us. I have met with remarkably few atheists. One woman said, "you care for people", after I said a prayer with her when her husband died suddenly.

In my retirement I preach most Sundays and conduct funeral services, usually for families with no church connection. Invariably I read First Corinthians Chapter 13 as the lesson. It covers every situation – suicides, murders, separations – and I endeavour to remind those present of the loving kindness of our heavenly Father. "Now abideth faith, hope, love, these three, but the greatest of these is love.'

The Shorter Catechism says, "Man's chief end is to glorify God and enjoy Him forever". I believe that God has shown us His heart of love in Jesus, who is the true and living way.

I believe we are called to love God, to follow the Christ, and to love our neighbour – anyone who needs our help – and render any service we can.

**FROM MRS DORIS M. BAILEY**   *Hemel Hempstead, Hertfordshire*
*2 November 1990*

I believe in a caring God. Not a God who is an insurance policy against falling ill, or meeting with trouble. We are all human, and expected to take life's woes as well

as its joys. But to have a *caring* God close beside us –
this is what matters.

May I give a long ago instance of His caring? Soon
after the war, things still in very short supply and
rationed, we moved to Portsmouth, buying our first
house. Until next payday, I was literally without any
money.

The children set out for school, and the five-year-old
asked, "What's for dinner, Mum?"

"Eggs and chips", I replied, knowing I could rely on
my hens in the back garden.

"Oh, not again!" cried Trevor. "I'm asking God for
fish and chips. He won't expect us to have eggs again!"

I went into the house. Twelve lovely eggs . . . and
nothing else. I hated shattering the child's faith.

A knock on the door, and an anxious woman stood
there.

"I hope you won't think I've a cheek asking, but I
hear you keep hens . . ." Diffidently she went on to
explain that her sick husband needed fresh eggs in his
diet. "Could you possibly sell me some?"

She looked at me anxiously; I returned her look joyfully. She went away rejoicing with her dozen eggs and
I sped gleefully to the local shop to buy fish, and got
home to find another egg ready for the batter!

A caring God? I'm SURE of it, and now, over forty
years on, I still find He cares in a practical way.

FROM MR D. C. GRADDON                   *Dymchurch, Kent*
                                        *20 November 1990*

Jesus spoke to Thomas: "You believe because you can
see me. Blessed are those who have not seen and yet
believe." (John 20:29)

From that day, Thomas has been held out as the first to reject the resurrection until he received absolute confirmation direct from Jesus himself. Poor Thomas, he was given a very heavy burden to carry to eternity: Thomas the Doubter. Yet it is not difficult now, after 2000 years, to appreciate Thomas' failing. He had just passed through what must have been the most traumatic experience of his life: his great leader had failed and had been crucified. All Thomas' dreams lay in shreds. Would we not have all reacted the same way?

Today, we have that 2000 years of experience behind us and I believe that although we cannot see Jesus enclosed in the flesh of man, he is totally within us, around us, and caring for us.

I know that the media would have us believe that all around us is pain and hate, and that strength is might. Good is not news, would not sell papers.

I believe one must look beyond this limited vision, and then all the good appears: the thousands of little kindnesses, and large ones: a smile in the street, someone offering a helping hand. These suggestions of good in the world only scratch the surface, but good outweighs evil, over and over again.

The evil comes from those who cannot or will not allow their hearts to open to Christ within them, or have never been taught that they are each a tabernacle with Christ living within them. Our prayers should be for them, our actions of goodness towards them.

FROM MARGARET EVANS                    *Southport, Merseyside*

I believe in the continuing creative energy that activates the universe. Surely it is within the experience of most of us that this creative energy is LOVE. Since the cosmos is one whole, it follows that there is a divine spark of this love in each of us. Some call it "that of God". We name it what we choose.

I believe that this divine spark can rise, and has risen, to a flame in some great minds and spirits, so that they have spoken to us through the ages, and made this a better world to live in. In simple gratitude, we should try to see that it is better still by the time we leave it.

Of course there are times when the flame of love burns low. Even Jesus was subject to temptation. Some giants, like Jacob, wrestle all night with their demon. The legendary Achilles fought a long battle with his demon through another dreadful night, and made a fatal decision. He dedicated his life to the wrong kind of strength, that which injures others.

Some, like Job, are subject to long-standing afflictions, and face a lifetime of deprivation or pain. For most of us there is the danger of growing callous, self-centred or envious – "How do the wicked prosper?" – then we are near to snuffing out the light of love.

But I believe we are closest to our creator and creation when we are tending that light, seeking out the light in others, and finding it.

FROM PETER TORJUSSEN                    *Godalming, Surrey*

I believe in God, who holds us in the palm of His hand. He made us for Himself and for Heaven, to live for ever with all we love.

Such Faith is a free gift not given to everyone, but there for the asking: something to be treasured and nourished by prayer and good works. Our Trust lies in a merciful God who will pardon our weaknesses.

We need never fear the present or future, but keep trusting and never stop trying.

Caring is all-important, because it will save all who practise it, even though Faith and Trust may be wanting.

All who will for others their highest possible good, and serve others in any way, do God's work on earth and, come the end, will be with God.

Getting older and closer to meeting God, Faith and Trust may falter, and worries about ourselves and others may weigh heavily, but we must persevere, keep believing, keep trusting, keep caring, assured that whatever troubles arise, we'll have peace of mind amidst seeming chaos.

This inner peace will keep us smiling in the face of adversity. Fear not. All is well. Our God rules.

FROM MISS MURIEL HALLIGAN        *Bexhill-on-Sea, East Sussex*

I believe in a loving, living God who cares deeply and personally for me and for every other member of the human race, who has ever lived and ever will live.

I think of myself as the little sparrow which cannot even fall to the ground without our Heavenly Father knowing it.

I believe that if I continue to love my Father, to trust Him as a little child trusts his father, to endeavour to do His will at all times, then one day I shall be joyfully united to Him in heaven for all eternity.

I believe also that while in this world we must show our love for God by loving our fellow man – whether it be the tiresome old lady next door, the cheeky child across the street or the grubby beggar who asks for 50p for a cup of tea. I believe we must have a cheery smile and a warm welcome for everyone we meet, looking at them with the loving glance we would give to Jesus if we were to meet Him.

I believe (in spite of much evidence to the contrary) that there is some good in every person and we must search for, appreciate and love this good.

To sum up, I believe in LOVE, love of God, of one's fellow man, and of all God's wonderful creation.

**FROM PETER ROE**                *Ambleside, Cumbria*
                                       *31 October 1990*

Christ explained by word and deed what we need to know about God. In essence, He told us that God is love.

But God works through people, and it is therefore our privilege to be channels through which that love reaches our fellow humans – IF, and, only if, we are willing to allow ourselves to be used that way.

I have tried to be such a channel of His love, and have found I have been repaid tenfold by the love that has come back to me from those around me. Perhaps my attempt has spurred others to be more loving. Certainly, they have spurred me.

This love brings me a contentment, an inner calm, which allows me to be at peace with myself and with the world. I can face the future in the sure knowledge that I have nothing to fear either from life or from death.

My only sadness is that there are so many millions who do not share that peace, or experience that love. But it is never too late to learn – to learn how to believe, how to love and to be loved. All you need is the DESIRE to say "I believe".

FROM MRS MARGARET THORN *Polegate, East Sussex*
*5 November 1990*

"God is Love" was the text which hung over many an old person's bed when I was a teenager, but as my empty head was filled with the kind of love I read about in romantic novels, I simply could not understand this text.

At about this time I also found I could no longer say the Creed when I went to church with my father, so as soon as I left home I became a lapsed Christian – not an atheist or an agnostic or a humanist, because I just did not think about religion at all.

But when I was in my early forties a friend sent me a little booklet which I have treasured ever since. It is called "The Greatest Thing in the World" by Henry Drummond, and is based on 1 Corinthians chapter 13. Among other things, the booklet translates St Paul's spectrum of love into nine simple ingredients – Patience, Kindness, Generosity, Humility, Courtesy, Unselfishness, Good temper, Guilelessness and Sincerity.

I have tried, not always successfully, to live up to these guidelines but it is only now, some forty years later, that I have become aware that these really are the attributes of God, and therefore God *is* Love.

None of us know what really happens after death, but I believe that there is nothing to fear, as the Spirit of love, whom we call God, will take good care of us and our loved ones.

**FROM JAMES ROTHWELL**                    *Carnforth, Lancashire*
                                            *6 November 1990*

In a hilltop village of the desert region of south-east Spain is a little shop. As I entered, it was audibly obvious that lunch was being enjoyed behind a partition. A young lady appeared, and I apologized for disturbing her meal.

"De nada," she said, "almuerzo esta muerto." ("Not at all, lunch is dead"!) My face must have shown surprise at this colloquial way of describing the end of a meal, for the girl smiled and used the more formal word "finito".

She, of course, was most anxious that we should be able to communicate so that we might do business together.

Which set me thinking about the arguments about the newer forms of worship, and how some people regret the passing of the majesty and dignity of the old. Perhaps we miss the point that we need to find the right words, new or old, colloquial or formal, to bring those who are in any sort of distress to a communion and communication that can lead to relief. The sick, the bereaved, the worried, the underprivileged, the heart-broken, the drop-outs – all need to communicate through others with a Saviour. It's the business of love that matters, not the words.

Sometimes we need to find the words so that we can seek to be sustained in order to practise that business of love. There is a simple prayer that we can use at any time, anywhere. It is a prayer that really works:

"Help me to live as one who has been with you, Lord Jesus. This I ask for your love's sake. Amen."

"Consider yourself . . . one of us"

**I believe . . .**
everyone should be welcomed into
church

(Church ministers are often bothered about how they
should answer the needs of the many people who come
along to church to be married, or to have their babies
christened, but never appear at any other time. *Saga*
letter writers reflect a variety of views.)

FROM MRS B. FRASER          *Henley-on-Thames, Oxfordshire*
                            *(in* Saga, *July/August 1991)*

I believe that our churches should welcome anyone who
wants to use them, however rarely.

I was lucky enough to be invited to two weddings
recently, one in a local church, another in Norfolk. Both
couples are young and, like the majority of our popu-
lation today, are not regular churchgoers. Nevertheless,
they all felt that they wanted to be married in church –
"It would mean more to us," one of the young brides
explained. But what different attitudes the two couples
met with.

The vicar of the Norfolk church welcomed the couple
and was only too happy that they wanted to be married
in church. He saw it as a chance to forge a link with
them and with others in the congregation who would
not normally go to church.

He said, "I am anxious that this young couple here

today and all their friends should feel as welcome in this church as those who come regularly."

Our local church is not so generous of heart. The couple who married there were cross-questioned as to why they wanted to be married in church and made to feel they were doing something wrong by asking.

I know which couple is more likely to return to church, and isn't that what we should all encourage? We can all try to be good shepherds and gather in stray sheep. They may break out again but isn't it better that they know that we will welcome them back at any time, not reprimand them for having been away?

(But here is a very different opinion, by Mrs Kellock):

FROM MRS R. A. KELLOCK          *Cattenham, Cambridgeshire*

I believe very strongly that the Church should not baptize, marry, or bury people on demand.

Years ago, at the age of nineteen, I married in church . . . and yes, I believed in God (so does the devil) but that's as far as it went. I had not time for Him in my life and heart.

Having been christened and confirmed, I really thought these made me a Christian. It lulled me into a false sense of security.

Then, thirteen years ago, at the age of 45, God met me in a wonderful way. I was shown that I am a sinner, that I needed to repent of my sins and to ask Jesus into my life and heart.

After my conversion, I couldn't help wondering why no-one had put forward the simple steps needed for me to have faith in Christ.

The only valid reason for wanting a church wedding

is because you are in fellowship with God, through Jesus, and seek His blessing on the union. This should be made very clear.

Surveys do not bear out Mrs Fraser's assumption that these people will return to church at a later date.

I would like to invite everyone to attend church (any denomination) any/every Sunday, where they will learn why God sent His Son to this earth – and then, if they will seek Him with all their heart – they will find Him. It is never too late.

FROM E. WELSH                            *Cookridge, Leeds*

So Mrs B. Fraser, Henley, thinks churches should welcome people to use them *rarely*. In the meantime they have to be supported by the regulars. Bills have to be paid, repairs, heating, etc.

If everyone used the church *rarely*, when they wanted, the church wouldn't be there. It is very sad to see these beautiful buildings closed down because of lack of support.

(But for Jim Simpson it was a rare visit to his local church that led him to a deeper faith.)

FROM JIM SIMPSON                       *Stockport, Cheshire*
                                           *(in* Saga, *May 1991)*

I can hardly be said to be an early convert to Christianity, since I was confirmed on my sixtieth birthday, 15 years ago.

It happened almost by accident when I attended morning service at the invitation of our vicar to hear a special sermon he was to preach. I had expected to be able to get out of the church without having to stay for the Communion Service which was to follow. I was unable to. And for the first time in my life I found myself experiencing the full glory of language, and the majestic panoply of a Eucharist.

I knew at the time what St Paul felt on the road to Damascus, and could not escape the power that drew me. Nor have I missed attending such a service every week since then. It took time to overcome my scruples, but I was led gently to writers who helped, through arguments that convinced me, and to a realization that what I was learning was truth.

My beliefs have been strengthened by many attendances over the years at a monastery in Mirfield. To live among such men who have devoted their whole lives to God, and to share in their observances, has humbled me and taught me much.

Five years after my conversion, my wife died of a malignant cancer. If I had not, by then, learned the power of faith and prayer, I should never have been able to overcome the loss of a lifetime partner.

(I was interested in Florence Broomfield's reason for not attending church – it's because she's a feminist!)

FROM MRS FLORENCE B. BROOMFIELD *Skelmersdale, Lancashire*
*5 November 1990*

I believe that the God, whom I love and worship, loves me so much that He would have sent His son just to redeem me. His love has sustained me throughout my life, so that even in my grief at the death of my 47-year-old first husband, my greatest fear was that my faith would diminish, and my prayer was Mark 9:24.

Through all the vicissitudes of normal life, He has heard my prayer.

. . . I know that His grace covers all my deficiencies, including an anger that makes it impossible for me to attend a church service because, as a feminist, I feel totally excluded by the male-imposed structures.

God understands that I cannot bear to be exhorted to "brotherly love" when I see the injustice of which men are capable, and He will give me strength to overcome these feelings of anger and exclusion, and to protest against injustices and to do whatever I can to alleviate the wrongs caused by the wickedness of men.

. . . With Julian of Norwich, I must believe that "all shall be well" but with the proviso of 2 Chronicles 7:14.

FROM MRS HELENA WILSON        *Henley-on-Thames, Oxfordshire*
*5 November 1990*

I lost my husband two years ago very suddenly and unexpectedly – it's been a tough road since, with the inevitable ups and downs.

Whilst in America this year I requested and received full immersion baptism. This has had a most positive affect upon me. Firstly, personality-wise, I feel very calm, balanced, more resilient, eager to learn, eager to do, eager to participate. I am more accepting of things I cannot alter.

AND very importantly, I feel part of God's family, NOT an outsider. I have no doubts, no arguments, but an acceptance of FAITH that ensures I am NEVER lonely. God is ALWAYS there to listen to my prayers, to forgive my mistakes, to help me in need.

WHEN one believes, and when one has faith, then obviously one will do one's best, whatever the circumstances. When one is in doubt, but able to pray, then one will be strengthened.

With a strong belief in prayer, goes a strong desire to "Get it Right" – be it deed, attitude or "saying the right thing at the right time".

To be part of God's family is warming and embracing – to be outside God's family must be a chilling prospect.

FROM ERIC FISHER                    *Canvey Island, Essex*
                                         *8 November 1990*

Having gone to a Church of England school as a young child, I was introduced to the basics of Christianity. As I grew older, I did not adhere to the instruction that I received, although much of it remained in my subconscious mind to be revived from time to time, when faced with varying temptations. I never attended church for many years and failed to resist those temptations, turning always to the secular attractions.

Four years ago I walked into my local church, and felt instantly a sense of belonging. Last year, whilst on holiday, in another church the minister said to me, "I hear you have a strong ministry where you come from." I believe that to be so.

We have active bible and prayer groups, and currently are following a clergy-led Back to Basics Christian course. What is encouraging is the number of young people who are taking up the challenges which I so lamentably neglected all those years ago.

I have learned through experience that God answers prayers. Not always directly, or as soon as the troubled heart would wish. In his wisdom he answers in a way that is right for the individual.

As an example, God may not remove the trouble, but

will give believers the strength to overcome it. It is only when we give our heart and mind to belief that we will recognize God in our life. All else falls into place. Knowledge, Wisdom, Patience and Love for one another, fall into place.

I ask myself, "Where was I when God wanted me? Where would I be without him now?"

"I am the Resurrection and the Life" saith the Lord.

(Another thing that worries many people is the number of different denominations there are in the Christian Church, and how divided we are. But here are some more hopeful ways of looking at it.)

**FROM MISS LOIS M. BARBER**               *Leigh-on-Sea, Essex*

Some people are concerned that there are so many different denominations in the Church. This has never bothered me, because I've always thought of the Church as an army, with different regiments. Each has its own particular characteristics and traditions but all are equally important in the work they do.

There are the "Sappers" – down-to-earth, practical people, doing not very glamorous jobs in not very attractive surroundings. I would equate them with the Salvation Army and the Quakers.

At the other end of the spectrum there are the regiments of Guards, involved in colourful ceremony and ritual. In between there are varying shades of belief and practice. The important point is that, as in the army, each regiment is united in loyalty to Queen and Country, so each denomination is "one in Christ Jesus".

In the First World War, in the trenches, some men

who were about to go "over the top" said they would like to take Communion. There was no bread and wine – only biscuits and lemonade. There was no padre, but my uncle, who was in the R.A.M.C., happened to be a Methodist lay-preacher.

He said it was the most moving experience of his life.

The amount of water you use in baptism doesn't matter any more when you are under a baptism of fire! All the arguments about who may or may not give Communion are irrelevant when you don't know if you will see tomorrow or not.

**FROM JOHN SWEETMAN**                    *Basingstoke, Hampshire*
                                          *21 November 1990*


## Confessions of an Ecumaniac

"I believe in the Holy, Catholic Church." I have been asserting my belief for sixty years, but the words do not mean to me now what they meant when I was young.

The Church is Christ's Church; it is Holy because it is His, and it is Catholic because "catholic" means universal, and that is what He intended it to be. Jesus also intended His Church to be unique, "That they all may be one" and for all men, this total inclusiveness is essential.

It is not easy to hold this concept of unity in practice. In the first decades of the Church's life men shouted, "I am for Paul", "I am for Cephas". Human failings have often led to hatred and misery; for most of my own life there has been difference and dissension but I do think that things are changing.

The ecumenical movement is a sign of the Holy Spirit

at work in our world as we begin more and more to understand that the beliefs that we hold in common are far greater and more significant than those matters that have for so long kept our man-made sects apart. There is now an imperative laid upon all Christians that they should continually strive to bring about the Unity which they must desire, and it is under that compulsion that I am proud to call myself an ecumaniac.

## "Love changes everything . . ."

## I believe . . .
### seek and ye shall find

(For many people the great Billy Graham missions of the '50s and '60s was a turning point in their lives.)

**FROM MRS MURIEL WELLS**                   *St Columb Major, Cornwall*
*11 November 1990*

When I read your reply to "IDEAS EXCHANGE" asking for 250 words on "I believe" my mind was at once filled with words, proverbs, verses from cards collected and saved over many years. However, with pen poised and thinking hard, I realized that all the ideas flowed only after I started to believe.

I had answered a call in the late fifties at Wembley Stadium, and read afterwards that there were thousands there, but I know as I walked forward, I was alone. That voice was only calling me.

My belief, faith, trust, call it what you will, has been tested many times and I have not done half the things I have promised. I have also thrown down the gauntlet and yet HE has never left me. How often have I said to the Lord, when things have gone wrong: "WHY? WHY? WHY?" And yet when I have been blessed, have I always said "Thank you"? NO – NO – NO.

Looking back, my life has been directed right from the crusade. Prayers have been answered, promises from Scripture kept. I am not a scholar, and you may find many faults in my writings, but this I know: the Lord Jesus Christ died for me, faults and all.

As I am a person who writes as they think, and my many letters to friends and relatives show I have a grasshopper mind, I am glad that HE keeps His promises to all who believe, and no more words are required.

FROM V. E. PAPMEL                                  *Willesden, London*
                                                   *13 November 1990*

Since my childhood I have always believed in the existence of God. Despite arguments to the contrary, this has always seemed perfectly reasonable; much more so than believing that blind chance brought about an intelligent and well ordered universe. True that there is much that is evil in the world, but God has given mankind free will and man has turned from his Maker.

By the time I had reached the age of 30, I did not need anyone to tell me that there was something missing in my life, but then I went to a Billy Graham Crusade meeting at Wembley Stadium. There I realized for the first time that I had missed the mark, and come short of God's standards, but despite this, God had sent Jesus to give His life on the cross to pay for all our sins. God was offering to me and to all a free pardon, if we would only put our complete trust in Him. That was more than 35 years ago, but the reality of that step of faith is still with me.

I know that what I have received from God through faith in Jesus Christ is not self-effort but the undeserved grace of God. The Bible tells me of His wonderful plan of redemption and of His great love. Life still has its ups and downs and I sometimes get things wrong, but I now know a God who answers prayer, who brings healing.

(For Raymond Ward, of Crawley, "Conversion" has gone in the reverse direction!)

FROM RAYMOND WARD                    *Crawley, West Sussex*
                                           *7 November 1990*

As a child, in rural Cornwall in the twenties, I attended the Methodist chapel like everyone else. My father was a local preacher, and my mother taught in Sunday School. It was this awareness of the general acceptance of religion, that led indirectly to my "conversion".

It was towards the end of the summer in which I became seventeen. Some Four Square Gospellers, who were holidaying in the area, had been invited to take the Sunday evening service. At the end, when we were seated with heads bowed waiting for the final prayer, the speaker asked those who wished to "declare themselves for Christ" to raise their hands.

Seated where I was, I could see little of the congregation; but assumed most would be raising their hands. The preacher duly thanked God, and concluded by asking those who had declared themselves to remain behind. Only then, as the rest filed out, did I realize that I was one of only two who had responded. The others were already "saved".

One of the gospellers approached me for counselling. He must have thought me very unforthcoming; but I was already beginning to realize that the part of religion that had most significance for him, and presumably my parents and the others, had no meaning for me. I emerged to the congratulations of family and friends, and never revealed to them what had happened.

That was nearly sixty years ago. I have never repented of my "conversion". It was as significant a step in my life as if it had been the other way around.

Surprisingly, it made very little difference to my basic beliefs. The Protestant work ethic, and feeling for my fellow man, has proved more durable than the concept of a supreme being. I have valued my early knowledge of the Bible, and am glad that I grew up familiar with the language of the Authorized Version, and with traditional English hymns.

My friends still tend to be Methodists or Quakers. Our attitudes to life and social issues are very similar. When it comes to "faith" or "God", I find I have no common ground of understanding. But I do not envy them the faith I cannot share.

FROM MISS J. LOGAN *Glasgow*

When I was young, I attended Sunday School, where the teachers cared about their scholars. I was taught that God made the world, and me as well.

He loved me, but hated my sin. Because of this He sent His Son, the Lord Jesus, into this world, to live and die for my sin. As a sinner I had to acknowledge Him as my Saviour, and He would forgive all my sins.

I was unwilling at that time to make this decision, but thought a lot about it.

Then when I was a teenager, a visiting preacher came to the church I attended to speak at the Sunday Services. One evening he spoke on the Great Judgement Day (Revelation 20:11) and as I listened, I knew I had to make my decision. Towards the end of the service I quietly bowed my head, and earnestly prayed "O Lord, save me."

God heard my prayer, and peace filled my heart.

I have recently learned a text from Romans 10:9:

"If thou shalt confess with thy mouth the Lord
Jesus and believe in thine heart that God hath
raised Him from the dead, thou shalt be saved."
(KJV)

This gave me the assurance that I needed, and through
daily bible reading and prayer, strengthened my faith.

He has been my refuge and strength through life,
and now that I am nearing the end, I know that the
Shepherd who saved me and kept me, will lead me
through the valley to the better land.

FROM MRS P. PENNINGTON                    *Haslemere, Surrey*
                                          *10 November 1990*

Yes, I believe. Even as a small child saying my prayers
I believed, but when I was in my late 30s I began to
feel there must be something more than we were being
told, so almost in desperation I prayed about it, and I
shall always believe that about three weeks later I
received the answer to that prayer. "Divine Healing and
Evangelistic Meetings" were to be held in the town for
a week.

I made a real commitment of my life to Jesus Christ at
the first meeting, and although I didn't ask for healing, I
was healed of colitis, which I had suffered from for
three years.

After the meetings a church was started in a tin hut
which I went along to. I didn't understand at that time
what Pentecostal was all about, but I accepted it was
biblical.

About nine years later I did seek a further blessing,
when an invitation was given. I went forward at about
8.30 one Sunday evening. All I can say is I came back

to earth at 9.50. For over an hour I was completely lost to the world. I was completely flooded with love and joy.

That was twenty-three years ago. This was not a one-off experience, whatever the circumstances this inner peace is always with me.

As the hymn says:

> For none can guess its grace
> Till he become the place
> Wherein the Holy Spirit makes his dwelling.

Jesus said, "Seek, and ye shall find, knock and the door shall be opened unto you."

Yes, I believe. There is a saying "It's better felt than telt." (This is so.)

FROM MISS J. GREEN    *Alcester, Warwickshire*
*April 1991*

"I believe – help Thou my unbelief." This prayer has remained more constant and meaningful to me than any other throughout a lifetime of vacillation between conviction and doubt.

In common with many people, I suspect, the questions to which there appear to be no answers have niggled away in my mind, and being unable to sort it all out, it is all too easy to let things slide and, like Scarlet O'Hara (in Gone with the Wind), say, "I'll think about it tomorrow."

But the extraordinary thing is that whilst the answers may not come, slowly a realization dawns as one's experience of life progresses. Some even will spark off a glimmer of perception which produces a gut reaction which says, "Never mind the why and wherefore, I just *know*."

Sadly, many people deliberately shut out these reactions but truly I believe that everyone has the opportunity to "seek and find" if they would but have the courage and will to do so.

It does not depend on one's childhood upbringing or environment. It *is* possible to hear God's voice – not in terms of hearing voices – but in our innermost being. When our conscience disturbs us that surely is when the message comes directly to us.

I firmly believe also in an evil spirit – how else can such terrible deeds be perpetrated which go beyond any feeling of decency or sensitivity?

So, when temptations come along – in whatever form – it is only by calling on that Deity to which we can respond, be it the Christian God, Muslim, Jewish or whatever, that we can achieve the strength of will to succeed in resisting, and with each success become more able "to believe" and thus obtain sufficient Faith to acknowledge a Divine Being and persist in the prayer "I believe, help Thou my unbelief."

FROM MRS DORA DOYLE                    *Ormskirk, Lancashire*

Today I had coffee with an old friend. She is 83 and has arthritis, which has almost crippled her. Basically she is a happy woman, but the illness has made her seriously depressed.

"Can you tell me," she said, "if life has any real purpose, and if it does, how can I find it, because I've reached the end of my tether."

I said I thought the way you look at life dictates the way you will act. Rather than wondering if there is a purpose to life, I think one should look for one, perhaps in work, or a hobby, or travel, or in family and relationships with friends. Man's essential need is to find God, and I believe one can seek God in this way.

Attending Church and doing good are only part of the Christian commitment. Two thousand years ago Jesus said: "Ye must be born again." I think a thousand religious exercises amount to nothing compared with the miracle of rebirth.

But this is perfection, you may say, and how is that possible without teetering on the edge? Don't you feel it is a matter of seeing a dawn light, and not the full sun? Knowing what a marvel that dawn light is, illumining every part of the mind. Other thoughts from old habits will arise and must be dealt with so that the power of pure consciousness may stand.

"You've got a friend . . ."

## I believe . . .
God answers prayer

(At the time when many people were writing their "I believe" columns to *Saga*, war in the Gulf was at first threatening, and then became a reality.)

**FROM HUGH SANSOM**                    *Tunbridge Wells, Kent*
*15 November 1990*

I don't pretend to understand prayer – but I know it works. In reply to a heckler who said that all "answers to prayer" were just coincidences, William Temple said, "All I know is that when I pray, coincidences happen; when I don't pray, they don't happen."

Jesus taught his disciples to pray and he even told them to expect God to answer: "Whatever you ask for in prayer, believe that you have received it, and it will be yours." (St Mark 11:24)

Most of us take photography for granted. We can't explain exactly how a picture is reproduced first on a piece of film and then in a colour print, but we enjoy taking photographs, and eagerly await the results. They may not always be quite what we expected, and they may have taken longer to come back than we hoped, but there is nearly always something to show our friends. Is that just a coincidence?

I believe we should pray about little things that worry us, as well as about big things. St Paul told the Christians in Philippi, "Don't worry over anything whatever;

tell God every detail of your needs in earnest and thankful prayer." (Philippians 4:5, J. B. Phillips)

At times of crisis in World War II our leaders in Church and State called the nation to prayer, and God answered our prayers. With the present threat of war in the Gulf, should we not as a nation pray to God for a peaceful solution to be found? I believe that he can answer that prayer too.

**FROM MRS OLIVE LEONARD**                    *Lancing, Sussex*
                                             *3 November 1990*

I believe that somewhere within me is the Holy Spirit, if only I can squash this inner, undesirable, self-willed "me". But how do I know which is the "me" and which is the Holy Spirit, when stopping to listen for an answer to prayer?

"Listen and God will speak to you." But are the first thoughts that come into my head really the Holy Spirit moving me, or is it some evil force – the Devil, perhaps – pushing his way forward?

The problem seems to me to be that, over the years, I have witnessed at least two episodes where apparently devout Christian people, in authoritative positions, have said or done positively evil things, obviously believing them to be instructions received via a "hot line from God". The results have been that the people affected have suffered abominably.

If I feel strongly about something, should I act and become a "stirrer"? If so, am I a "stirrer" for Christ or for some evil spirit? It is so much simpler to sit back and do nothing, but, like many people, I have a strong desire to help others for Christ – it's just so difficult to know how and when.

I can only hope that the voluntary work my husband and I have been moved to undertake since retirement is really for Christ, and that in no way are we doing it for any reward – either in this life or hereafter.


FROM MRS A. ALLINSON                          *Christchurch, Dorset*

The other day I visited a friend who lost her husband very suddenly three months ago.

"The night before he died," she told me, "we had a most wonderful hour of prayer together."

Looking at her serenely smiling face, I had a rare insight not only into the closeness of their fifty-three years of marriage, but into the meaning of prayer.

She spoke, too, of the support of her church congregation during the early days of her bereavement.

"I felt I was being rocked on gentle waters and I knew they were praying for me."

Too often prayer is something we resort to only in times of trouble, but it is a great source of strength and peace at all times, the channel through which God's love comes to us and an experience that we can share with those we love.


FROM MRS K. M. ALEXANDER                          *Totnes, Devon*
                                                  *6 August 1991*

I BELIEVE in miracles! My oldest and dearest friend of 55 years was widowed two years ago. With the reduced income, increasing cost of living and especially ever-increasing rent for her apartment, she had decided regretfully that she would have to find somewhere else to live. This was making her very unhappy, because the apartment held such happy memories for her.

For all of her adult life she has been a tireless worker for her Church, for various charities and helped endless people in any way that it was humanly possible, giving her time and money when and wherever it was needed.

I have recently had a letter to say that, out of the blue, she received a fairly substantial sum of money, a legacy from an aunt, which will enable her to stay in her apartment, hopefully for the rest of her life. I cannot think of someone who deserves it more.

It is said, "The Devil looks after his own" but here is proof that God looks after HIS own also, and that prayers ARE answered. I am not a religious person, but knowing what a good and faithful servant my friend has been, it has certainly given me food for thought!

FROM MRS N. MACMILLAN                                    *Birmingham*
                                                         *13 May 1991*

God hears and answers prayer. In 1941 my husband was in the Air Force and I was in a bedsitting-room in Ayr, Scotland, no proper home. Our first baby died, and I was told I would not be able to have any more children. The only glimmer of hope, the surgeon told me, was I *might* be able to have one child by Caesarean birth, but only one.

In my Bible reading, I read a psalm a day, going through the psalms systematically through the years, always finding help and blessings to suit every need. I read Psalm 113, the last verse:

He maketh the barren woman to keep house and to be a joyful mother of children. Praise ye the Lord.

I knelt down in that bedsitting-room, and laid my finger on that verse, my Bible wet with tears, and asked God, if it was His will, to fulfil that verse in my life.

Ten years later, my husband returned home safely, we had a house back in my home town, Birmingham, and two lovely sons, both born naturally. Truly God had answered my prayer.

But God does more than we ask or think. In 1954 He blessed us with a lovely baby daughter, again a natural birth. "Praise ye the Lord."

FROM MRS IRENE MUNN                  *New Barnet, Hertfordshire*
                                           *14 March 1991*

I believe that God, loving and all-powerful, does hear our prayers and out of love is always ready to give help and guidance in our problems. But – I also believe that there has to be complete trust and faith on our side.

The Bible records how Jesus asks of the suppliant, "Believest thou that I can do this thing?" and unless we can answer in true and trusting faith, "Lord, I believe" then we obstruct His will.

It is not easy to have complete trust and faith, for fears and doubts are always too ready to beset us, but I do know from experience that once I have been able to empty my mind of all doubt, and trust solely in Him, that help in rich abundance has always been given to me.

His way may not have been the way I would have chosen or desired, but once His guidance has been accepted and followed in faith (for we can, I think, choose to ignore His advice), then the way the problem has been solved has been solely for my good, as I believe He desires. And in prayer I acknowledge and thank Him.

> "Believest thou I can do this thing?"
> "Lord, I believe."

FROM MRS M. SNAPE                    *Colchester, Essex*
                                      *10 November 1990*

I believe God has guided me over all of my 75 years. Looking back to my teens, when I was entirely alone in the world, and not constantly in touch with Him, I know that I was kept on "the straight and narrow". The pitfalls I could have fallen into horrify me on reflection.

Even today, over small decisions I have to make, I find by hesitating and praying I come up with the right answer. Sometimes I am impulsive, but that too seems to bear fruit. I care enough to carry out my convictions.

We all have an inner conscience, and should listen to it, whether it be belief in God, or whatever religion or creed. I pray fervently against war and all the tragedy it brings.

FROM NORAH M. BETI                    *Glasgow*

I believe in the necessity of prayer. As our bodies require nourishment, so too do our souls. We need food *every* day, so we need prayer *every* day, to enable our spiritual lives to grow and develop. We should put aside a little time each day to be alone with God; to tell Him our needs, and our love for Him.

To really love someone, you must know them intimately. Prayer is our way of fostering this intimate relationship.

A wonderful way of showing God our love for Him, is by loving Him in those around us. We should train ourselves to see God in other people. If we could see their good points and overlook their less lovable qualities we should be well on our way to a perfect relationship with God!

Finally, and joyfully, I believe (despite the wars and wickedness, the immorality and Godlessness which blights this world of ours today) that God did reveal to that great mystic and spiritual writer of the fourteenth century, Julian of Norwich, "But all shall be well, and all shall be well, and all manner of thing shall be well."

FROM MRS JOSEPHINE ROBERTS *Tarland Aboyne, Aberdeenshire*
25 October 1990

I believe with Julian of Norwich that "All shall be well and all shall be well and all manner of thing shall be well."

If we believe in the resurrection of Christ, then nothing, but nothing, can defeat us in life. Because we know that the healing power of the living Christ walks with us every breath we breathe, and that that Great Power works according to God's laws, not ours.

Sometimes we older people can feel utterly heartsick, bewildered and alienated by the chaos, tragedy and sadness we see all around us. We feel a sense of guilt that in some strange way we are to blame for the horrendous heritage of misery we are leaving our children. We feel helpless, and that there is absolutely nothing we can do.

And yet, we do have the marvellous tool of prayer.

The Lady Julian of Norwich never left her tiny hermit cell in Norwich. Yet the power of her prayers for the suffering people of the world were answered in many astounding ways.

From the moment we lay the burden of our fears, doubts, anxieties and heartbreaks at the feet of Christ and earnestly beg help for the world, and forgiveness for our own sins of omission, something marvellous happens – we experience an almost instant gift of peace, calm and certainty in the knowledge that God is in control, now and for ever.

We begin to see afresh the great good that has evolved over the centuries. We remember how astounded we were by the caring and generosity of ordinary people during the last national or international disaster. We know from quite recent history that people are better fed, better housed and, despite present clamour, better educated. Health care alone would seem a daily miracle to people of past generations, whilst the mentally handicapped are treated with respect and compassion. And so much more.

And so, very quietly, the Holy Spirit works gently and surely in us all, as the centuries roll on, and we are assured that, in God's good time, man will be made whole.

Julian of Norwich was very close to God, in love and charity, and I believe with her that: "All shall be well, and all shall be well, and all manner of thing shall be well."

FROM M.D.T.                                        *Bath, Avon*

Yes, I believe. How could I not? When I see the tiny crumpled face of a newborn baby, or smell the perfume of a rose after rain, how could I not believe in a Being who fashioned these things?

Many years ago my husband was dangerously ill in hospital, and not expected to live through the night. He came through, and everyone said, "Wonderful! Penicillin!" But I knew that God had answered my prayers. Nineteen years later, in an horrific road accident, my husband and son survived their serious injuries, though others lost their lives.

Our world is truly a wonderful place, but these are troubled times and many people fear for the future. How comforting it is to know that there is always someone to whom one can turn at any time for advice and help and love. Tennyson put it marvellously:

> Speak to Him for He hears,
> and Spirit with Spirit can meet –
> Closer is He than breathing,
> and nearer than hands and feet.

I hope that I will never forget to say thank you each and every day for the blessings of children and grandchildren, for health and strength, and above all for a loving and devoted husband.

FROM MRS ANNE ALLAN  *Marlow, Buckinghamshire*
*5 November 1990*

Clergy and various people like to make things difficult. We live and we die. I am 93, and would not be afraid to die tomorrow, but no I am not, God is with me every single minute of the day, and I am a firm believer in that.

God knows the day you are born and the day you die. The majority of people do not have any faith.

If I have problems, I ask God, then someone comes

along, and I get the answer. Patience is the answer. I may not get whatever it is immediately, but I have proved again and again, it will come, and it DOES!

FROM MISS W. SYKES                    *Halifax, West Yorkshire*

I believe that nothing is impossible with God, and I believe in the power of prayer. I have met people whose lives have been changed by the prayers of other people, and I have met others who have been miraculously healed either through their own faith or that of others.

We all go through times when we feel low and depressed, or we may need help in coming to a decision, or knowing what to say. If we lay ourselves open to God and pour out our concerns and worries, we find peace, and so often the next day help is at hand.

Many folk are lonely, but Jesus said, "I am with you always." Loneliness vanishes if we find someone else on their own and make friends.

Many of us, as we grow older, may fear about the future when perhaps we may lose our faculties, and we can no longer cope on our own and will have to leave home. Here are some words which encourage me: "Do not be afraid of tomorrow – God is already there."

I commend to others the verses of the hymn written by John Greenleaf Whittier, which begins:

> All as God wills, who wisely heeds
> to give or to withold,
> And knoweth more of all my needs
> than all my prayers have told.

which sums up my faith.

FROM JOHN CANSBERG                    *Oldham, Lancashire*

I am a retired electrical engineer. My age is 80 years and I'm a widower. I lost my wife in 1982. We were together 44 years.

During my working life, I came up against many problems and I found that I was able to solve them with the help of a prayer. I'm *not* claiming any miracles happened, but something gave me the strength to overcome the difficulty.

I am a great believer in the power of prayer, and I have a daily "chat" even now. As a result of this, I believe I live a happy and contented life, to enjoy my hobby. I am an artist, and I believe.

# PART THREE

## *Seed-time and Harvest-time*

Our dear and loving village church has a service every year in the summer for the Blessing of the Animals. Well, I know that many country churches do, but I boast that ours is as major an event as the Opening of Parliament or Cruft's or the Olympic Games! We hold it in the churchyard, and take our own folding chairs, (well, they don't *have* to be folding, but most of them are) and believe me, the arrival of the animals at Noah's Ark was *nothing* compared to our presentation on Animals Sunday!

The folks arrive, either being tugged into the churchyard by bounding dogs on leads, or carefully carrying little baskets containing a mouse, or a pair of guinea pigs; the odd pony crops greedily and noisily away at the long grass along the edges of the graveyard wall; cats various; hens; rabbits in small hutches; goldfish in jam jars – you name 'em, and we'll produce 'em! It's glorious – especially if it's a sunny day; dogs barking and growling at each other and a gay, well-met feeling amongst the zoo-owning parishioners. Rather like the Royal Garden Party, really (in a very small way, of course)!

At the end of the service coffee is brought round and everyone puts something in the small servietted basket that holds a card which has printed on it in ink: COFFEES – THANK YOU!

One year a young lad – oo, about ten or eleven I think he would be – brought his large ginger tomcat.

They looked quite a picture because the lad's hair was the same colour as the cat's!

I cannot speak too highly of our vicar, Roger. He goes to each animal and puts his hand on its head and blesses it with the love of God, adding its name. In our case, Jan takes Tess and Patch who, belonging to an Acting Family, both give performances of Oscar standard! The expression on their faces is so saintly, or "martyr-like" would be more like it, that I always feel like laughing.

Any road up (as we are supposed to say in Lancashire, but never do!) on the occasion I speak of, the ginger-haired boy and the ginger cat were sitting together on the grass, the cat lying behind a gravestone that over the years had sunk into the soft earth, leaving only the half-circle top of it in view (do you follow?), but just high enough to hide the cat from Roger's view.

The blessings were completed and Roger returned to the Victorian marble-topped washstand (which we use as an altar on this auspicious occasion), quite unaware that he had missed blessing the ginger cat. There was such a sad, neglected look on the ginger-haired owner's little face, that I called out (because *anybody* can at our church):

"Excuse me, Roger, but you've missed a little Christian cat behind that gravestone!" Roger immediately came over to the cat, and gently putting his hand out to bestow his blessing on its little ginger head, was rewarded with a cat-hissing-and-spitting-scene unparalleled in history! I must admit the performance was received with "full house" laughter that any actor or actress would have welcomed!

This July a BBC film crew came along to film it all (I *told* you we were big-time! My mother would have said, "Well, now you've hit the top! You've nothing left to fight for!") Anyway, I hope to be able to show you part of our happy, loving service on *Praise Be!* next spring.

This little story doesn't carry any important message, but I hope you liked it! It introduces another group of *Saga* letters which are all about finding God in our beautiful world of animals and nature. Some of them are about how much harm we humans have done to God's creation through greed and materialism, and, as always, "the media" comes in for its full share of criticism. But I notice that in some of the letters people say that nature programmes they've seen on television have been for them the starting point of seeing God's hand in creation. So television can't be all bad, can it?

For far and away the most people, the beauties of nature have led them to say "I believe".

## "All things bright and beautiful"

## I believe . . .
we find God in His creation

FROM TERRY WALSH                    *East Looe, Cornwall*

When I see all the different birds looking for food in my garden, it makes me thank God, for I do believe all life is created by Him. When I see my roses come into bud, and watch apples form each year on my tree, I again thank God, for I believe he created all nature.

I cannot understand people thinking everything in the world happened by chance – all the different plants, animals, birds, insects – all just happened to be, without any help from anyone.

I feel sad when I hear people who don't believe take pleasure in bringing God's name into question. They ask, "How can God allow all those poor children to starve to death?" and "How can your loving God allow a 'plane to be blown up, and all on board killed?"

I don't have any answers, I only believe that God does exist and that He is a God of love, not hate. He does not go about blowing up 'planes, nor does He make people starve to death in time of famine. There has to be some other answer, some man-made cause. God is not a terrorist.

As I grow older, I rely more and more on God to help me through each day, and while I am far from perfect, I do try.

FROM ELSIE HEARNSHAW                    *Eastbourne, Sussex*

My husband and I have just come back from visiting our son, who is doing voluntary work in Zimbabwe. What amazing animal and bird life we saw! Then the gorgeous sight of the jacaranda trees, which were out in full bloom, with so many other shrubs and plants of every colour and hue. Also seeing the great spectacle of Victoria Falls, which was an experience indeed.

And when I think that the God in whom I believe, and to whom I can speak as my heavenly Father, is the creator of all these things, this adds such a dimension to everything. As the old hymn puts it:

> Heaven above is softer blue,
> Earth around is sweeter green,
> Something lives in every hue
> Christless eyes have never seen . . .

This God in whom I believe is a God who is not only all-powerful, but loving – interested in even me. This He has made so evident in that He sent his only Son into the world to be our Saviour. So I tell Him all that troubles and concerns me; and what relief that is, because, being who He is, He is able to do something about it.

Like most *Saga* readers, I am no longer in the bloom of youth, but through believing have experienced His help in every area of life.

To have such a Friend has given life another dimension, and through believing, I know I shall spend eternity in His presence.

**FROM MRS MAY HAYWOOD**　　　　*Chichester, West Sussex*

I am very fond of the passage in the new Communion Service:

"All things come from Thee, O Lord, and of Thine own do we give Thee." It makes me feel small and conscious that I really have nothing of my own to give, and yet this does not lessen the joy of the Father.

It puts me in mind of the years when our children were small. On special days they would creep out into the garden early, and appear with posies for our delight.

Plant cuttings are much the same. You beg a bit from a friend's garden; in time it becomes a sturdy plant; someone admires it, and you generously give them a piece. It is not really yours to give – yet you have nurtured, fed, watered and loved it, so it has absorbed something of you. You wonder about its future life: how many hands, careful and casual, will it pass through? It may change its character with different treatment, different soils and position. Each small piece passed on will have lost or gained something; stories of its origin will be told as people stroll round gardens. Some may even go full circle, with a piece passed back to its original owner. I wonder if she will know it. If she does, she will feel as I do:

"All things come from Thee, O Lord, and of Thine own do we give Thee."

**FROM D. SHEARMAN**　　　　*Clapham, London*
*5 November 1990*

I believe because I see God's almighty hand all around me in the beauty of nature. The tiny seed growing to its full potential, the numerous and different kinds of animals, down to the smallest insect. And what about the marvels of space – that myriad of stars, all much bigger than planet earth, the galaxies rushing along at fantastic speeds, all in the order of things? You can't but acknowledge the presence of a much greater Being than man himself.

I find God in prayer, and having prayer answered, the greatest force this world will ever know.

Think about Divine healing. Apart from the "laying on of hands", a surgeon can perform an operation, but it's only through God that the actual healing takes place.

Did you know that every prophecy in the Bible has, so far, come true? How could those men have known, without Divine revelation?

The joy and happiness that one experiences in meeting Him at the Holy Communion or in a few moments of quiet meditation, are beyond description.

That is why I believe and trust in Him.


FROM MRS NANCY SCOTT                    *Malvern, Worcestershire*
                                              *9 January 1991*

The flowers are so beautiful at Eastertime. But none so beautiful as the modest, frail little snowdrop just coming into bloom in my garden. To me this clump is always a miracle, because it appears where some previous owner of the garden had decided that a concrete path should be, and so within this stone tomb the little plants were sealed.

But come the time of Easter, and a wonderful thing happens – through cracks in the stonework appear the stems, rising up stronger and stronger, and each delicate bell as it opens seeming to ring a peal of victory –

"See! I have overcome death, I have risen from the tomb!"

And every time I look at this small miracle of life, I seem to touch, in some small part, the deep emotion Mary must have experienced when she met her Master, Jesus, in the garden, risen from the dead; and my faith and hope are renewed.

(Some letters were about how pet animals, too, can tell their owners about the love of God – something which I heartily endorse, as you might have guessed by now!)

FROM MRS M. W. EASTON                    *Woburn, Bedfordshire*
                                          *29 November 1990*

There is an afterlife, and I believe I have had proof of this. Several years ago I had a very old, loyal and dear friend. She was a black labrador, named Glenda. We seemed mentally in tune.

As the years passed, she began to walk slower. Arthritis, the vet told me, and later she began to suffer from diabetes. She still enjoyed some quality of life, so I decided to help her as much as I could, until this was no longer so.

Eventually that day arrived. Sadly I telephoned the vet, and prepared to wait with my friend. It was early in the morning, and the vet did not arrive until lunchtime.

Before then, at approximately 10 am, I knew the moment was near. For the first time I could see she was really suffering. I was near to tears. As I put my arms around her, "O God, if you're going to take her, take her now" I begged.

Suddenly, with arms clasped around her, her eyes glazed and she gave three great shudders, and died.

Almost immediately I experienced a feeling of intense relief; then a sense of well-being; followed instantly by a sensation of utter bliss.

Those were not my thoughts, not my feelings – I was in tears. How could it be other than her release from this painful world and her entry into a wonderful world on the other side that I had experienced? I know she lives on.

FROM RITA SPRINGTHORPE     *Sheffield, South Yorkshire*
*27 November 1990*

I believe that God is interested in everything that concerns us – no matter what it is.

In the Bible it says that God cares for sparrows. He also cares about cats! I have a biscuit-coloured cat called Gold. Now Gold would only eat a particular flavour of a certain brand of cat food. All was well, until the company stopped making this particular flavour. He refused to eat any other kind of cat food. He just went up to his dish, sniffed at it, and walked disdainfully away. He miaowed at me, but wouldn't touch his food.

Well, besides being cross about wasting money, I was also feeling upset. I had visions of him starving to death.

I knew that God could control His creatures. When Elijah was hiding by the brook, God sent ravens to him with food in their beaks. My friend and I prayed to God about Gold's refusal to eat, and committed the problem to Him.

I bought some cat food, and put it in his dish. He came towards it, sniffed, and went away.

"Please may he eat it, Lord," I pleaded.

He came again and sniffed. "Eat your food, Gold," I

said gently. He licked it. "Good boy," I coaxed. He looked at me, and then ate a little. He ate more.

"Thank you, Lord," I said.

Gold now eats the different varieties of this brand of cat food. Yes – God certainly cares about our concerns.

(Some *Saga* readers were even inspired to send their replies in verse!)

**FROM MRS LESLEY TALBOT**                    *Stockport, Cheshire*

Is it really true –
That the tiny humming bird,
Feathered with gold and with wings of roseate hue,
Flies from Mexico to Arctic cold to sip the honeydew?

Is it really true –
That lobsters file across the ocean floors,
Defending themselves from predators
By forming circles with their claws?

Is it really true – That elvers, born in tropic seas,
    emigrate to England;
For seven years they grow and yearn,
And then – themselves to breed – return?

Is it really true –
That of all this great Creation
Man buries his instincts deep,
Submits to humble domestication and
Subordinates his powers to civilization?

Is it really true – Man has no compass in his head,
But works to earn his daily bread,

His feet stuck firmly in the sod,
His heart and mind yet seeking God?

Given dominion over all the earth,
Is he now the least of all,
Instincts atrophied at birth?

And when he dies, if granted faith, what next?
Will he find proof beyond belief and all pretext?
Living, he knows only Faith,
Dying, he steps beyond, and knows Belief.

In a better world . . .
May he discard sophistication
And return to Nature, and re-creation?
Can this be really true?

FROM MRS WINIFRED OSBORNE                    *Ryde, I.O.W.*

I believe – not with the best reason, which is trust,
But I believe because I must.
Because if this life here is all
At times I find no sense at all.
I know there is beauty of the flowers,
I know the fragrance of the showers
Falling softly on the earth,
Calling all plants to new birth.
I know the majesty of the oak,
I know the kindness of most folk.
I know the glory of a summer breeze
Singing softly through the trees.
I know the early morning dew
And the rainbow shining through.
I know the vastness of the sea

And all the love that's shown to me.
I know also that I've been blessed
Above all by the glory my eyes can see
And appreciate the beauty all around me.
But this I know and stronger still
That something more my heart must fill,
Some greater need than all these things
The knowledge that these all – God brings.
Without this knowledge firmly tight
I could not face the still of night.
So I believe because I must –
Oh Lord above, fulfil my trust.

**FROM LIONEL ROSE**　　　　　　　*Lymington, Hampshire*

## Testimony

There is a glorious peace about this place,
Alone, with all its beauty I embrace
The cloudless sky, the whispering placid sea.
Are these foretastes of future artistry?

Tonight I shall commune with my own heart
(The shield that keeps the mind and soul apart)
And with the gift of age and thought implanted
Give thanks for every further moment granted.

There is a Voice outwith my mortal mind
Without Whose words, these words I would not find;
That being so, this my endorsement and my brief
To that Great Love – unwavering belief.

(The complexity and wonder of our universe is the starting point for many people's meditations. For most, it is a sure sign of a Creator.)

**FROM MRS DOROTHY HEDDLE** *Bexhill-on-Sea, East Sussex*

I look up into the night sky, at the moon, the stars, the planets, and I believe someone keeps it all up there.

I look into the television screen at an undersea documentary, and marvel at the variety and beauty of life in that waterworld, and I believe there must be a Mind behind it all.

I look at the incredible beauty and symmetry of a snowflake, and I have to believe in a Master Mind who designed it in the first place. I call that Mind: God, the One who made infinite variety in flowers, trees, animals, insects and the human race.

And when the mind boggles at the consideration of outer space beyond this universe, I then look in the one Book that tells me most about Him, and I find His greatness humble enough to take on the form of a man, in order that we might the better understand something of what He is like.

I believe what I read about this divine Man in that Book, because the things He is recorded as having said open to me a whole new dimension of living, and I find by His triumph over death that He gives me a new quality of life here and now; life in the power of His Spirit; and however far short I fall of His ideal, I know He understands, forgives, and promises me a wonderful destiny when I no longer have need of my earthly body.

FROM C. WEST                                    *Bristol, Avon*

I believe – What? That the Bible is the Word of God.

I believe that God is the Creator – Why?

As I look at the miraculous intricacy and beauty of even the tiniest flower, the wonder and strength of a tree, and hear of the marvels of the workings in the animal kingdom, and as I learn of the way in which our world depends on such extreme precision and balance for its very existence – only a marvellous Creator, not a chance happening, could do this!

So, I believe in His Word, and though there are many things I do not understand and often question, yet through it all one truth is clear, that God's love for us is deep and wonderful, for:

> God so loved the world that He gave His only begotten Son, that all who believe in Him should not perish, but have everlasting life. (John 3:16)

And His love is so great that Jesus died, a terrible death, for me – and for you. To "believe" in Jesus is not just a passive, casual belief, but asking Him into your heart and life, to be your Saviour and your friend. It's a personal, living fellowship, that brings joy, love and purpose into a human life, a certainty of His presence and the power of His Spirit within you in this life and through to the life eternal:

> Lo, I am with you always. (Matthew 28:20)

As I look back on my life, I can trace His guiding hand, not always in the way I had prayed for, but in His way for my best, His love and comfort in the dark days, and countless blessings. Yes, I believe!

FROM WILLIAM SIMMONS                              *Fife, Scotland*

Humanity, incapable of creating any new thing, has to rely on using that which already exists. An automobile, for example, is simply basic raw material refined, moulded and assembled to a new form or shape. As evidence of its maker is clearly seen by that which is made, any insistence on personal visible proof of the maker and means of production is merely supplementary.

Similarly, all living creatures can only create additional new life, each by their particular means of reproduction.

Francesco Redi demonstrated that all life derives from preceding life, not from dead inanimate matter. Madame Curie's discovery of radium revealed that matter has not eternally existed but, at some time in the distant past, came into existence.

Despite that built-in natural prejudice against unseen authority and the spiritual limitation of the human mind, one cannot rationally deny the eternal existence of a first cause, a creator and lifegiver, unless the origin of life, physical matter and laws governing and sustaining the universe can otherwise be accounted for.


(But as in all good discussions, there are always some people who disagree!)


FROM JOHN BINGHAM                              *Northampton*
                                               *2 April 1991*

Entering my seventies, my understanding of God's existence has survived many heart-searchings and questionings over the years.

Great prophets of the past have propounded their theories according to the times and events in which they lived, yet none of the religious orders thus far evolved have provided me with a real answer to this mystery.

Yet do we need this indefinable belief? There is no doubt that religion offers a wealth of comfort and support to its followers and is thus to be encouraged, yet for me the void remains unfilled.

We live on a minor planet around a minor sun in a minor galaxy of the universe, yet have the typical conceit of mankind to imagine that its creator has picked us out for special treatment. We are products of an evolutionary plan and should appreciate the importance of this, and be satisfied.

We live here but briefly, and when we are gone we are soon forgotten, as one day the planet on which we live will be gone too. The only morality which makes sense to me is to do as many useful acts as possible, in this short time allotted, and hope for the best.

FROM H. HAPSTON                          *Dereham, Norfolk*
                                          *3 November 1990*

I do NOT believe in any of these gods, and this is why.

The Sun is just a G-Type star. G-Type stars are the most common in the galaxy. Our galaxy is one of millions in the universe.

What utter conceit it is to assume that one small planet going round one G-type star in one typical galaxy of millions of such is the sole beneficiary of the attentions of one particular being who claims to have been responsible for all the universe.

More people have been tortured and murdered in the

name of one god or another than for any other reason. If you need a Big Daddy in the sky to run to I respect your right to one, but if you quote any of the bibles to me as proof of there being a god, I shall only laugh louder.

**FROM ALAN R. CORBETT**    *Dronfield, Derbyshire*
*27 November 1990*

I believe that we are born into a living world of beauty and of complexity, yet of ordered development, beyond the comprehension of man. Man has lived in this world for an infinitely small part of its existence, and may yet prove to be a species which becomes extinct, as other species have before him.

Man has, throughout his history, sought the source of creation. Recognizing the magnitude of the creative force, he has developed the idea initially of gods, and then of a single God. I believe that the concept of God existed only as man's awareness of language developed. Thus we have created the idea of God in the image of supreme, perfect and omnipotent power, which man imperfectly resembles.

In the prophet Jesus we have a magnificent example of how man can best live in our human society. To claim that he was born the son of a God perhaps detracts from his outstanding personal qualities of charity, humility and leadership. As we live on after death in the minds of those who knew us, or who learned of our acts, so too does Jesus.

I believe that we know so little of our creation, and that there is much more to be learned and then to be understood. Perhaps those religions and sects which insist that they have the only and final answer to creation and our lives do us only a little service in the end.

There is a marvellous mystery which may one day be answered if we continue to question – let it not be lost in myth and dogma.

(But you might know, the vast majority of letters were from people who, like David Hatton, in spite of all these questions, can still say, "I believe".)

**FROM DAVID HATTON**                    *Sudbury, Suffolk*
                                         *11 November 1990*

I believe, despite "modern science".

A microchip achieves miracles: the "pen" at the check-out can also check the stock, and move a trolley to replenish shelves. Yet this is the product of man's thinking. Man himself is a greater miracle.

I sit on a chair. Is it solid? No. It is an empty space but for minute particles, or waves, of energy. The invisible world is more real than the visible one.

I see martins returning from Africa to the same area, the same eaves, as last year, and believe their homing devices should be called miraculous.

I watch a natural history programme and marvel as I see man tracing the path of evolution. But man cannot say *why* these things happen, *how* the in-built processes came to be. Man is but discovering paths a creator first laid down.

And the start of it all? Scientists speak of a "Big Bang" many millions of years ago. The author of Genesis presented his ideas in a word picture: the picture presented by today's scientists is not dissimilar.

I look into a pond. Fish live out their lives there, but

know nothing of my world, my thoughts. Yet those are real, even though completely out of reach of the fish's thought and experience. It is wise for man to realize that there can be infinitely greater things beyond the little fish pond in which we live.

Some great modern scientists find Christian belief still possible. So do I.

## "And only man is vile"

## I believe . . .
Our own materialism destroys the beauty of God's world

FROM MRS P. J. CROFT          *Farnborough, Hampshire*

I believe, though I confess my belief is severely tested in the cruel materialistic world of today. A world in which morals, values, discipline are all losing their significance and importance as each day ends. To believe in the existence of a compassionate, all-powerful God is a great comfort and a strong support in these troubled times. Faith can be likened to a lifebelt – it keeps one afloat when way out of depth.

Further, I believe that one of the hardest tasks a committed Christian has to undertake is the ability to accept, without rancour or a "cry for vengeance", "man's inhumanity to man". It is practically impossible to remain rational and forgiving when reading of child abuse, rape, paedophiles and other terrible, unlawful acts. The immediate response is "An eye for an eye, a tooth for a tooth", not "Turn the other cheek."

"To err is human, To forgive, Divine." To err is most certainly human, but I believe that to practise forgiveness, we must remind ourselves constantly of the Divine example: "Father, forgive them, they know not what they do."

"Father, forgive them",
Is hard to say
When you sort the remains
Of a bloody affray.

"Father, forgive them",
Is hard to say
When you number the dead
At the end of the day.

"Father, forgive them",
Is hard to say
When you view a world
They colour so grey.

"Father, forgive them",
Try hard to say
The words that He said
On His dying day.

FROM MRS R. HODGSON                    *Pickering, North Yorkshire*
                                       *6 December 1990*

I am not an avid Bible reader, but several things spring
to mind, such as "Money is the root of all evil" and
"Do as you would be done by."

Doesn't the first saying really mean that greed is the
root of all evil, and, to do as you would be done by,
surely means that we should treat others as well as
we ourselves want to be treated, and to be caring and
compassionate to all species?

Greed can cause wars, famine, and all manner of
problems, from petty crimes to dreadful, ecological dis-
asters. I believe that if we want peace in the world, we

shall have to restore harmony, and to do that, we shall have to accept that although we may be the dominant species, that does not give us the right to plunder and destroy by our greed and lack of care. We shall have to use good husbandry if the world is to continue supporting life.

Where does religion come into this? I expect you will ask. If we believe there is a God, and that God created the earth, then it can only be right to look after His creation and all other species, not just ourselves. Don't you agree?

I believe that the Bible does have some sound commonsense in it to point us in the right direction.

Those two sayings go a long way to promoting peace if we follow them. The result of not following these messages is too horrible to contemplate!

FROM MRS O. N. T. CONNOR                    *Ashtead, Surrey*
                                                   *4 November 1990*

I believe that God has given us a beautiful world to live in, and by greed and carelessness we have abused our responsibility and are fouling and destroying it and its inhabitants.

Those people and companies greedy for money and power put out alluring advertisements to tempt our youngsters to drink or drugs or promiscuous sexual behaviour, careless of the havoc they wreak on human lives. Others hack down the rain forests or pollute the seas with no thought for our responsibility to the God-given order in Nature.

In spite of this, I also firmly believe that there is an innate goodness in most people, which gives us a strong impulse towards the generosity of giving and caring for others, even when it demands the sacrifice of our own selfish desires. We have seen this recently in the large amounts of money raised for the poor of the Third World – for unknown people whom we are never even likely to meet, but who need help.

I believe that God has given each of us a special purpose in life to fulfil, which no-one else can do. We may never know what it is in this life, only in the next, so we can only try to hold fast to the age-old values of honesty, decency, respect and concern for others as best we may.

Above all, a loving and generous heart to serve God and our neighbours is of priceless worth.

MISS V. MEADOWS                      *Birmingham*
*8 November 1990*

It is true that people are too busy to take up the challenge of discussion of the faith that guides us daily, but the strenuous and strident lifestyle portrayed by the media does not encourage thought or meditation, and certainly does pander to the careless acceptance of modern "affluence" as being the norm!

My generation was nurtured in a hard school, where one learned to appreciate every happy experience as a gift, willingly shared with family and friends. Gratitude for any favours was part of the code of conduct.

Rampant materialism had not reared its ugly head and "designer labels" had little significance – one's worth as a being of integrity was of more importance! In today's strife-torn world, immense pressures, seen and unseen, give conflicting impressions which are the enemy of the seeker of serenity and spiritual certainty.

As *Saga* members of mature outlook, we resist

"trendy" blandishments and turn to a quest for the meaning of existence. Professor Barclay taught that suffering through loss, doubt, disillusion and despair is transformed by our loving Creator into strength to endure in the knowledge we are not alone. Famous characters, including poets, musicians and artists, inspire us to glorify the living presence of our great Teacher with the guidance of the Sermon on the Mount.

The path is hard, but we are confident of reaching our desired heaven.

FROM MRS IVY SHIPTON                           *Lancaster*
                                        *10 November 1990*

Ever since I was a small child I was conscious of a voice inside me telling me how I should behave. I may not have always listened, but throughout adversity, and many blows, I have now arrived in my golden years convinced more than ever that if we have love and faith, we can overcome all hurdles.

If you respect nature, and all natural things, you will find peace and harmony. You get back only what you give.

In the Middle East, Ireland, and places where terrorism occurs, surely people will realize one day that this is a fact?

Try smiling at a stranger, returning a harsh word with a soft answer, and prove that kindness has its returns.

Materialism is what is destroying our society today. Partnerships fail because sex and materialism rather than love seem to rule. Some children grow up without ever knowing what love is.

How many times do you hear it said: "behaved like

animals"? Animals do not mug, rape, riot or torture. If only we could have the simple faith found in creatures of nature, we would be more happy. Yet man destroys beautiful things like the dolphin, the seal, and the trees of our planet.

I believe there is no saintly man on a throne up there in the clouds who is going to reach out his hands and save us from destroying our planet by nuclear war or environmental pollution. The inner voice was given us, and salvation was put in our hands by a God force emanating from a world beyond this one.

"How great Thou art!"

**I believe . . .**
in signs and wonders

(For some people some things happen which they feel
can't be explained . . . I think you need to be Scots to
fully appreciate the beginning of Peter Mitchell's letter!)

**FROM PETER MITCHELL**

*Keith, Banffshire*
*19 November 1990*

I remember a time when a minister at school was talking
to some young people. He remarked that often he had
been asked if he had had a situation which proved to
him that there was a God. He said that when he was a
youth, he was playing golf with his one and only golf
ball. It landed in rough, and he could not find it. As he
was about to give up, something told him to look at a
place where he had not looked before, and sure enough,
there was the golf ball! "God had spoken to him," he
said.

One day, coming home for lunch, I suddenly found
myself driving off the road into the garageway. I had
never done this before, as I always parked on the road-
side during this time.

It so happened that while I was having lunch a car
had gone out of control and banged into a car which
was parked only a few yards from where I would have
been. My wife said I had listened to God.

You may say, "Why had God not spoken to the lady

who had parked her car which was damaged?"

Had she been spoken to, but had not listened to God? I believe that God does speak to us all, but sometimes we just do not listen.

I am not deeply religious, but my belief in God has never faltered, even when I have heard eloquent arguments to the contrary.

FROM MRS WENDY HAINES                   *Oldham, Lancashire*
                                        *3 February 1991*

During my time at school I was very impressed by the life of Marcus Aurelius, and he said:

"Our life is what our thoughts make of it."

So now, much later on in my life, I have learned that one should think clearly and cleanly, and never give the Devil a chance to get into our minds or actions. In that way God can get in to help us on the way.

During the War (with Hitler) we lived in Croydon, and when France fell, we felt that this was the end. But while wandering round the garden, feeling distraught and anxious, a white dove flew over our house. I felt a wave of peace come over me, and that the house would stand, and we would come through. We did.

Look out for the good signs in life, and you can pull through.

FROM MR G. E. WHEELER                    *Exmouth, Devon*
                                         *9 November 1990*

I firmly believe in the GOD of the BIBLE, and try to uphold the moral code derived from its teaching.

Any doubts I had of a God personally interested in me were dispelled about 6 o'clock one morning during the Blitz.

I was on standby duty, twenty-four hours on, twenty-four hours off, at Bexleyheath ARP depot. Being last crew out, I slept in my clothes, woke early and decided to find out if anything had occurred. I walked from the rest area in the reinforced building to the Duty Room.

As I stepped through the doorway a voice, sounding just like my Mother's, called "Gordon!" in a tone of alarm. I swung my foot backwards, and just at that split second a heavy steel girder and tons of concrete slid down, blocking the door. I believe there were six killed and ten injured by the delayed action bomb hitting the centre of the building. No-one else was awake in the off duty section, and I ran up to the top of the council yard to raise the alarm at the Danson Park Control room.

I believe God loves me personally, because He saved my life in time of danger. I also believe because He saves those that put their trust in the Lord Jesus Christ.

FROM MRS MURIEL C. UPLEBY          *Maidenhead, Berkshire*

I believe that I am made in the image of God, and that God loves me; but He knows my weakness, and sent His Son into the world to save sinners – so that includes me!

I believe that death is but the gateway to life through Jesus Christ my Saviour, the only Son of God. That belief gives me strength for today, and an assurance for the future.

In the past it has upheld me in difficult circumstances. After nearly four years in the WAAF as a conscript I returned to "civvy street" with a faith made stronger for its testimony.

When at death's door in 1958 I had a vision of the

Crucified Saviour hanging on the wall of my room. That was followed immediately by a picture of the Risen Lord passing by my bed. I still don't understand it, but it renewed my faith and gave me a wonderful sense of His presence through four months in hospital.

I believe that God is the source of my life and my hope for the future in a new heaven and earth. I believe the Bible is God's word to guide us into His kingdom.

## "Abide with me"

### I believe . . .
## God finds us in our darkest hour

FROM EILEEN GRAY    *London*

Despite experiencing two great sorrows in a short space of time – the untimely death of my husband and, more tragically, the loss of my younger daughter, who died of cancer when she was only thirty-four, I still believe in God and His everlasting love for us. I have a lot to be thankful for: a roof over my head, good friends, and the knowledge that when I depart this life I can look forward to being reunited with my loved ones.

Those of us who go to church reaffirm our belief in God by saying the Creed. It's a bit like declaring which side you are on! I feel the more people who believe in God, the more forceful the message will be. Evil is all around us, and it is up to those who believe to fight it with all their might.

I am sometimes asked why I believe, when there is so much evidence of tragedy and evildoing. It is not easy to convey an inner conviction in the face of media reportage, but good things are happening all the time, they just don't make the headlines . . .

I believe that the love of God will prevail eventually; I also know that, were it proved CONCLUSIVELY that God no longer existed, my life, and all that I am, would cease to have any meaning.

FROM MRS MARGARET MACKENZIE       *Hove, Sussex*
*13 November 1990*

I first began going to church in search of a faith and purpose for my life when I was about twenty. I came to feel that the Gospel was true, although I still questioned some aspects of it, and I still tended to go my own way.

A few years later, following health and personal problems, I had a complete nervous breakdown. After this, I felt that I needed to change, although how to set about it I did not really know.

After marriage and the birth of my son, I had another breakdown, and my faith was badly shaken. However, shortly after this I met some people who told me that if I gave my life to God, he would speak to me and guide me, and show me how to straighten it out. This I did, and I began to see what lay at the root of my problems, and what I needed to change.

Since that time, with God's help, step by step over the years, I have been able to overcome my many fears, and to think more of others and less of myself. I have also received a miraculous healing of severe and long-standing back trouble, and been helped through many other troubles and difficulties, including the death of my second child and the death of my husband.

I now live alone and after many instances of the Lord's help and guidance I can say firmly and with certainty: "I believe."

FROM MRS JOYCE MARRABLE       *Hatfield, Hertfordshire*
*8 November 1990*

Aged 65, I suffer from osteoarthritis in my spine and hips. It happened suddenly eighteen months ago and, having been a very active person, it was a bitter blow as my life style took a dramatic change.

However, with the help of an excellent G.P. I slowly came to terms with the situation; that is, until last August, when the arthritis trapped a nerve in my spine, causing numbness in my legs. On one occasion the use almost went completely.

I thought, "No, Lord, this cannot be happening to me." I was so frightened, and my fear knew no bounds. I felt so ashamed. However, I prayed, and I believe Jesus heard my prayers, because in a wonderful way I found great release.

Knowing I needed help, I talked with a priest who had helped me before. Very gently and lovingly Father took me into the Garden of Gethsemane where, when Jesus prayed, we are told a sudden fear came over Him and great distress; the beads of sweat fell from Him like drops of blood.

"You see," said Father, "Jesus, having experienced fear, understands your fear now. So share your fear with Jesus and lay it at the foot of His Cross."

I did, and a tremendous sense of peace filled my being. No, I did not experience a cure for arthritis but I believe I had a healing, for I have never experienced such fear again.

FROM MRS A. COLLEDGE                     *Tyne and Wear*
                                         *20 December 1990*

I believe that when we are in difficulties we are never alone, but Christ will come to us and support us.

I know this because, some years ago, my husband became very ill. We had just moved to a city, where I knew no-one, from a small town where I had many friends and family near.

One night my husband became much worse, and I telephoned the doctor. It went through to the emergency service who refused to come out. I felt desperate, as I was alone with my two children, who were just babies and not able to help.

I got up and went to the spare bedroom and lay on the bed. Then I thought: "Well, if he is going to die, he can die in my arms" as I knew he did not want to go to hospital. Then I felt a presence, and I felt peaceful. After that in all the troubles I had, I felt Christ was near at hand. At my right shoulder, to be specific.

Now things are better I do not have that strong sense of His presence, but I know that if things get difficult I need never be on my own. He is always near if needed by me, or anyone else, and this is a great comfort.

**FROM PASTOR L. PHILLIPS** *Bridgend, Wales*
*15 July 1991*

My wife and I have been Christians for over fifty years, and we have both found that our Christian faith has helped us in the most dire circumstances.

It was our sad experience when expecting our third child (which we hoped would be a boy, having had two girls), to find that the boy of our expectations would never be able to walk or talk.

While we have never been able to understand why this should have happened to us, we have also realized that, just because we are Christians, we cannot expect to be exempt from life's difficulties and troubles.

We found strength and help in the faith that we had embraced. Furthermore, we have had the privilege and joy to be able to help folk who have found themselves in similar circumstances to ours. Many, of course, had been turned away from the Christian pathway because of an experience they could never understand, and would never accept.

But we thank God that our experience has been that we have been grounded more deeply in our relationship with our heavenly Father, and brought closer to each other.

Why, you may ask, has this been the case with you? Simply because, first of all, we believe that in the end all will work out for good, even for our dear son; and then, because we realized that if ever we needed each other it was in the moment of difficulty.

As was the word of consolation to the great Apostle Paul, so that same word can apply to all who trust in God:

"My grace is sufficient for thee."

God's grace has been our strength and stay, and it can be the same to all who trust in the One who knows what is best.

FROM MRS M. FINNIMORE         *Exmouth, Devon*

Crete, April 12, 1989. A happy, uneventful flight from Gatwick, exciting taxi journey to our favourite resort, enjoyable meal at our usual taverna with old friends, bed, sleep, and BANG! My world fell apart. Almost as he awoke my husband had a severe stroke.

To myself I said, "I don't believe it!" Following a frantic journey to the nearest hospital eighty kilometres away, I sat by his bedside, helpless except for prayer.

I telephoned our daughter, who told our sons and our rector. From then on I felt surrounded by a deep warmth and comfort, knowing they were praying for us.

Gradually my husband's condition improved, and we were able to pray together. After two weeks we were flown home, and a period of hospitalization followed, during which we received Holy Communion and, when he was discharged, continued to do so regularly at home.

The happy day came when I was able to take him to church in his wheelchair, and we were able to take the Sacrament with our friends once more.

I feel I was always surrounded by God's love, and was quietly guided through my many problems. We continue our church worship together, walking to church with no wheelchair now, thank God.

In May this year we revisited Crete and saw the doctors, nurses and friends to thank them, and have since been to Oberammergau with International Church Travel to see the Passion Play. In April 1989, who would have believed that possible? I believe!

"Through all the changing scenes of life . . ."

**I believe . . .**
to everything there is a season

(This last theme in this section of the book is the changing seasons, how they affect us, and how they sometimes seem to mirror our own journey through life. We all develop our own routines, and have you noticed how even different days of the week can have a different "feel" to them?)

FROM MISS E. M. COUSINS

*Woking, Surrey*
*7 November 1990*

Although only recently retired I find the biggest difference is the precious commodity of time – time to stand and stare and contemplate, instead of rushing on to the next task waiting for attention.

There is so much to see and give thanks for: the squirrel eating a nut under a tree, a flower still blooming in a winter's garden, a shaft of sunlight . . .

We can say that we are in the autumn of our lives, but in that season there is great hope. There is a maturity springing from a lifetime's experience, and nothing can take that away. The leaves are falling, but on close inspection, next season's buds are lurking deep, ready to turn into new life in the spring.

Surely our God did not create all of nature to regenerate each year and leave us out! I find great comfort in comparing life to nature. We are born and flourish, either in a corner or openly for all to behold; all different shapes, sizes and colours. There are warm days as well as cold times, but all count for experience and memories. The longer we live, the greater our memories, and nothing can separate us from these.

Let us meditate on our living, not regretting any action which cannot now be altered, but with gratitude for the good times, and a hope for the future, as this life cannot have been for no purpose.

FROM DAVID DANIELS                    *Southport, Merseyside*

I believe that the way to grow old without really noticing the fact is to keep looking forward and planning ahead. It is comforting to have a storehouse of treasured memories, but those who only look back have lost the zest for living.

It does not matter whether one plans a wildlife safari in Africa, or a simple picnic in a field just a bus ride away. It's the looking forward, the planning, and the vision of the future which are important.

This may involve taking up a new activity such as painting, learning to type, cooking new dishes, or becoming involved in social work. There may well be an activity which you have wanted to try but have never actually taken the first step. Don't let fear of failure, or ridicule, deter you. If you want to do it, it's worth doing, and if it's worth doing, it's even worth doing badly if you can't do it well.

Treasure your memories, but keep looking to the future.

I recall one experience which remains vivid in my memory after all these years. It was in Glacier Valley in the Himalayas. Around me was the green meadow studded with colourful wildflowers. Facing me was the massive Kolahoi Glacier, which must have been inching its way forward through the centuries since the beginning of time. I raised my eyes to gaze at the snow-draped mountain peaks, pointing heavenwards, magnificent and awe-inspiring, against the backcloth of a clear blue sky.

In that one brief moment of my life, I glimpsed eternity. That experience is a treasured memory and, perhaps, in some mysterious way, was also a vision of the future.

FROM MRS D. BRADLEY                    *Whitley Bay, Sunderland*
                                               *14 November 1990*

I reached my eighty-first birthday a few days ago, and having lived through two world wars, I have had my share of ups and downs.

Life has not always taken the path I would have chosen, nor have I been able to follow my own inclinations and wishes in many aspects of my life. When I have been at a low ebb I have found the friendship and Christian love of my fellow churchgoers to be a great strength and "faith-booster".

Prayers have not always been answered as I would have wished. Sometimes I have doubted His love for me. But, on looking back over the bad times, I can see that strength was given according to my need. I was never asked to bear anything without being given the strength to face it.

I fail Him often, but He never fails me, and so I can turn to Him in my loneliness, my despondency and my worrying about what the future holds. With Whittier I can say:

Here in the maddening maze of things,
When tossed by storm and flood:
To one fixed ground my spirit clings,
I know that God is good!

FROM BARBARA M. THATCHER          *Helensburgh, Scotland*

I am in my mid-sixties, and have recently been ordained Deacon in the Scottish Episcopal Church.

I believe that as we grow older, we should not stop growing. There is always the danger that our faith gets stuck and stops developing: some adults still use the childish prayers – God bless Mummy and Daddy – that were once appropriate, but which should have been left behind in the nursery. Some still keep very unhelpful pictures of God in their minds – perhaps like a fierce, cruel schoolmaster.

I believe we should sort through these old notions, like looking through old clothes in the attic, discarding those that no longer fit, or would make us look like mutton dressed as lamb. They may have sentimental value and it may be hard to let them go, but – to change the image – we are still on our pilgrimage and don't want to be weighted down with out-of-date belongings.

To help us on our way I believe we should get hold of the most up-to-date translation of the Bible we can find, so that the old, old story comes across in a fresh, new way.

And as our journey draws towards its goal, I believe we should dump all the burdens of guilt and resentment and anger we so often carry. For God loves us just as we are. So I believe we should let go – and let God.

**FROM VICTOR L. SHELDRICK**        *Rotherham, Yorkshire*
*16 November 1990*

Pencilled in the margin of a hotel Bible were the words:

> My God, in His loving-kindness, will meet me at
> every corner.

I have found those hopeful words to be true. Life has many clearways, but also crossroads and T-junctions. It is *there* that we need help.

Before we reach the corner we can see the signpost. We cannot read it yet, but someone has prepared the way, and we go in faith.

What corner do we face? A spell in hospital, giving up our home, increasing weakness or disability? God has promised to meet us there. Shall we recognize Him in the hospital sister, the warden of a housing complex, the social services visitor, or a neighbour? As Browning wrote: "Supposing that friend should happen to be God".

**FROM TOM JENKINS**        *Rhondda, Mid Glamorgan*
*23 November 1990*

. . . A journey is always more interesting if beforehand we can have a glance at the map and see how the roads, railways and rivers run, to know something of the hills and dales, to get some mental grasp, some small explanation concerning what we shall be confronted with. The journey becomes easier and more enlightened if we can prepare ourselves before we come upon this and that on our onward way.

. . . I believe that from the cradle to the grave is

certainly a journey. May I also say I believe that this is only the first stage of the journey, and that we shall ultimately arrive at God's terminus, beyond the grave, which I believe to be far superior to any exotic location *Saga* has projected.

God's Book, THE BIBLE, not only makes the journey more interesting, but I believe, He has sent His Representative on before . . .

**FROM MRS MARGARET SYME**          *Clwyd, North Wales*
                                     *28 October 1990*

This morning I stood in our little thirteenth-century church, facing the altar, with the sun shining through the stained-glass window. We, the congregation, were saying the Creed – "I believe in God, the Father . . ." In my youth I recited these words, and the Lord's Prayer, mostly out of habit. Now, in later years, the words are said with conviction. I do believe in God, not as a benign Father Christmas figure, more like the Great White Spirit of the American Indians.

I believe in Jesus and his teachings. There are some verses in the Bible which say we are only travellers upon the earth, like Christian in *Pilgrim's Progress*, with all the sorrows and joys of the journey. And the best thing to do is to talk to God as the invisible companion at all times. To thank him when blessings come, and to ask for help and comfort when tragedy comes crashing down upon us.

Prayer really works – it is always answered, not always by miracles, and not always for what we ask, but God never lets us down. We are given strength to carry on. We are given the chance to learn life's lessons, counting our riches in the love of friends.

At the end of the Creed is the part which particularly affects us as we near the end of our journey – belief in the resurrection of the body and the life of the world to come. So Death is not the end, but just another beginning.

# PART FOUR

# *Life, Death and Eternity*

During the Second World War, if you were walking along London's East India Dock Road, you would probably have noticed the church with a notice outside which read:

IF YOUR KNEES ARE KNOCKING – KNEEL ON THEM!

as good a call to prayer as I've ever heard!

And perhaps plenty of praying is why nobody's knees seem to be knocking among the *Saga* letter-writers at the thought of reaching the end of their days. As long, that is, as they can arrive with dignity. I think many of us, like Doris, the woman I played in *Cream Cracker under the Settee*, have a bit of dread at the thought of spending our last days sitting side by side in a dismal row, being forced to sing "I'm H.A.P.P.Y." I'm sure we all pray that we can keep our sense of humour and our independence to the last.

When, a few years ago, I was playing the part of Ivy Unsworth, the old-fashioned undertaker in ITV's comedy series *In Loving Memory*, there were just one or two viewers, only a very few I'm happy to say, who seemed to think that we were "making fun" of death and bereavement. Nothing could be further from the truth, and I received many, many more letters from people who said the series had cheered and consoled them and even helped them a little to get over their sadness at the loss of a loved one.

What we were having a little gentle fun with in the series was the ritual of funeral arrangements, and the way most of us are not really at ease, dressed in our best clothes, with this very formal, solemn way we have to say our last goodbye to our loved ones.

I'll always remember a letter I received, when the series was going out, from a lady, who told me she had been travelling with her auntie in her uncle's funeral procession, when in the middle of a busy street the hearse came to a sudden halt right outside Marks and Spencer's, with smoke and flames pouring from the engine. Pandemonium! The coffin was removed from the hearse, with all its floral tributes on top, and set down on the pavement. Everyone started to rush around in a panic, and the fire brigade was sent for, and they were soon surrounded by men in yellow helmets aiming their hoses at the hearse.

She said she and her auntie were both sitting there, a bit shocked – especially as they were both thinking about how her uncle had always said he wanted to be cremated, but her aunt had insisted on burying him. Passers by stopped to look on in amazement, and she heard a woman say, "Ey'up! It's a coffin! It'll be Thora. I bet they are filming *In Loving Memory*. Yes! There's Thora in the car. Billy will have been sent to fetch a new hearse!" (She wrote to tell me this, because it had made her laugh, and then cry, and then she thought that her uncle wouldn't mind a bit, and would be laughing, too.)

This last part of our book gets right down to brass tacks, and there are letters about the Bible, Jesus, the three faces of God, other religions, but the last and largest section of all is about what *Saga* readers believe is going to happen after this life comes to an end. Well, once you've passed your three score years and ten – or twenty – you're bound to wonder, aren't you?

You'll remember that the person who started off this whole idea of an "I believe" column was Marjory Davys (with a "y" and an "s", kindly note), so we have put her own contribution at the top of this last part of the book. (My own bit is in here somewhere, too!)

FROM MARJORY DAVYS    *Newbury, Berkshire*
*14 November 1990*

I believe in a supreme spiritual Power, a righteous loving God. I believe that Jesus Christ was a true portrait or manifestation of the Power, and of its love. By his life and death he showed us what God is like, and what we ourselves should try to be like.

I believe that in each of us there is a breath, a spark, of God's Holy Spirit. If we desire it, that spark will direct our lives. It is what separates us from the animals, it is what makes each of us a living soul.

I do not believe in Satan as a separate identity. We are basically animals, and evil comes from our indulging our animal desires. I do not believe in the traditional hell, but I do believe that we can kill the Divine Spark and so cut ourselves off from God.

I believe Christianity to be the highest and purest religion, but I cannot believe that it is the only road to God. A just creator would not reject those who honestly believe and practise Judaism, Islam, Hinduism or any of the great religions.

The Bible is fundamentally an inspired book, but I do not believe that every word of it is true. It has been translated, edited and altered so many times, we cannot be sure that our present book says exactly what the original writers meant. Moreover, our knowledge of the world has increased so amazingly, that we cannot accept all that was written 2000 or more years ago.

I believe in prayer, providing it is real prayer, and not mechanical repetition.

With regard to life after death, I have no beliefs. I try to do what is right for the sake of the world and of other people, and for the rest – I will wait and see. I shall not have long to wait.

Lord, Thy Word abideth
And our footsteps guideth.

**I believe . . .**
God is in the Bible

(It'll help if you have a Bible handy while reading this next bit, because some people have given chapter and verse, but they haven't all written out the texts they are referring to in full.)

FROM MR W. G. FORD

*Brighton, Sussex*
*24 November 1990*

As a Christian, I believe that the Bible is the Word of God, and that it has total authority over anything men may teach. I believe that the only way to become a Christian is through the Lord Jesus Christ, who said (John 3) "You must be born again."

I believe that the Lord Jesus Christ will return again to this earth, as He said He will, and that Christians should consider the events in the world, i.e. the break up of the USSR empire and the gathering of the forces of the whole world in the Middle East, as signs foretold in the Bible.

I believe in Heaven and Hell, a coming judgement and the separation from God of all those who have rejected His salvation. The present trend toward unity is based on wrong ideals – Christ's Church is already one, in Him; attempts to gloss over man-made differences only hide the clarity of the Gospel, that deals with God's relationship with men and women, boys and girls.

May I pose the question: not "do we need women priests?" but "do we need priests at all?" – there being no further sacrifice to make?

FROM MRS MARJORIE TOWNER *Fleet, Hampshire*

I came to a personal faith at age 16 through a school friend taking me to a Bible class, where I heard the biblical explanation of sin and of God's remedy, through the death of His Son Jesus.

I was deeply moved that God should love me so much, and responded by dedicating myself to follow God's ways all my life. Like everyone else I have had several severe setbacks (mainly health problems) but I can truly say that after 51 years God's love still means everything to me, and worship on Sundays is a real joy.

My husband and I have based our life together on the Bible, using its precepts to bring up our three children and have found life full and rewarding. Jesus said, "I have come that they might have life, life in all its fullness." Living Christianity is not dull – church-going may be!

An added bonus to this full life is that I believe that there is a fuller and more exciting one to come.

FROM RENE AND ROD FRAMPTON *Amersham, Buckinghamshire*
*17 November 1990*

For my wife and me the Bible is a daily guide, and we find great comfort in its clear message that our welcome into eternity does not depend on how "good" we have been throughout our lives.

What is so wonderful is that "God so loved us that He gave His only Son, that each one who believes in Him should have eternal life." It was only Jesus who lived a holy life, which is why the old hymn reads

> There was no other good enough
> To pay the price of sin.

Jesus himself said, "I am the way, the truth and the life, and no one comes to the Father except through me." No one else could make such a stupendous claim.

This brings us to confession for the way we have failed to love the Lord with all our hearts, and our neighbours as ourselves, and to receive His forgiveness. Because of what Jesus did at Calvary, and not because of our achievements, we may confidently expect to live with Him for ever (read John's Gospel, chapter 14).

This prospect challenges us to live our remaining days seeking to put God first.

FROM COLIN BULL                              *Ipswich, Suffolk*
                                             *13 November 1990*

I was brought up in a Christian family and was taught to believe and live Christian values, but as life progressed I heard liberal theologians debunk the fundamental tenets of the Bible.

Is the virgin conception and resurrection of Christ a fact or a myth? Does it matter? Is the Old Testament fact or legend? Did God create the world, or is the theory of evolution true?

As these ideas were forced in my mind, my doubts

multiplied. Perhaps the Bible is not true; perhaps Jesus was just a good man; perhaps the Bible helps us lead a good life, but no more; perhaps there is no great Creator.

My Christian belief was beginning to disintegrate, but it was then that I decided to take the Bible on trust, and live *as if* it were true, and see what happened. Then perhaps I would throw it away.

What did I find? That faith works!

It soon became clear to me that Christ died for my sins, and in my place. He, the sinless one, atoned for my sin, and I knew that I was forgiven and saved.

Life took on a new meaning, and eternal life with him for ever was a certainty.

Would eleven disciples have suffered martyrdom for a myth? The Bible is true. Christ is the Messiah. And Almighty God is the creator of the universe.

How glad I am that I took that step of faith.

**FROM ROBERT LYTLE**
*Warrington, Lancashire*
*7 November 1990*

I believe that true religion is the most important of all subjects, and does good to all who embrace it. I also believe that false religion misleads, and causes anything from hurt feelings to mass murder.

How do we tell the difference between true and false? I believe that the Bible shows the way, with James 1:5 being a key Scripture.

I believe that true religion comes from our Father in Heaven, Jesus Christ, and the Holy Ghost, and that false religion comes from Satan and his many helpers.

The good news is that God the Father has more on His side, numerically that is. The bad news is that Satan is able to deceive even the very elect. The Bible says so.

We must test all things, and hold fast to that which is true. The Bible says that, too.

More power to your elbow.

**FROM MRS E. D. HEYS**                    *Wrexham, Clwyd*
                                        *21 November 1990*

How do I arrive at my firm conviction that Christ was God on earth?

He has told me so – in the Bible – and throughout all my life, by always answering prayers. So I say, as my Grandfather did, "He is tried and proved."

. . . The most urgent need for humanity today is to read the Bible. This is how we learn about our Maker. Then we go about our daily tasks with joy, in the conviction that we are greatly loved.

As we grow older there are fewer people who know and love us, but God knows me inside and out, and He is always with me as part of my being – the part which will go on after my body has perished.

It is not easy to talk of religious matters to those we meet, as there seems to be a great embarrassment in talking of God and things not seen. Material things are visible and humans are generally materialistic.

. . . I realize that I am stating my own views, and am sorry if I sound dogmatic, but I am so sure of my convictions, that I have difficulty in seeing other ways of believing!

**FROM WALTER AND ELSIE STREET**      *Romsey, Hampshire*
                                        *16 November 1990*

I believe the Bible to be the Holy Scriptures, inspired by the Holy Spirit, introducing us to the living God,

His nature, His councils, His purposes, thoughts and ways.

His love was manifest in giving His Son Jesus Christ to live, die and rise again for all who will "BELIEVE". (John 3:16)

The Christian life can be received and lived according to John 1:12:

> To as many as received Him (Jesus) to them He gives Authority to become children of God, even to those who BELIEVE on His Name.

This I have experienced to be real in a lifetime which is full and rewarding, and the best is yet to come.

**FROM ERIC WOOD**
*Southampton, Hampshire*
*22 November 1990*

Belief vitally affects behaviour, confidence, well-being, security and certainty of past, present and future. Both belief and source must be rock-like. We have God, creator of the vast universe, with its macro and micro aspects, Jesus Christ, and the Bible, God's guide for our life.

The Bible has hundreds of predictions of the life, crucifixion and resurrection of Jesus; and predictions of the Second Coming and conditions prevailing – many of which have already occurred.

There is also the epic of the Israel nation from Genesis to Revelation, and most of the story has been fulfilled, much during our lifetime.

Many maxims, warnings, rights and conditions are given for our benefit.

We have all failed God's standard, but He has given

us the remedy when we fulfil the conditions – help for all circumstances.

I had open heart surgery which went wrong, and am now registered blind and suffer from many defects, but there are promises for me.

We are able to contact Him at any time through prayer, and with help from the Bible. We must not allow the imperfections of Christians to deprive us of our God-given right of eternal welfare. The Nicene Creed, as recited in most churches every Sunday morning, reminds us of the foundations of our faith and hope for the future.

FROM MR R. BETTRIDGE                    *Winchester, Hampshire*
                                        *30 October 1990*

The Lord God made man from the dust of the earth, and breathed into him the breath of life, and he became a living soul. (Genesis 2:7)

God gave Adam a wife, Eve. The Devil tempted Eve, and they both sinned against God, therefore all born after were born in sin, therefore man's soul was dead, parted from God.

In due time Jesus Christ, God's Son, was born, lived approx 33 years on this earth, died on the cross to save us from sin and bring us back to God by the shedding of His Blood and was raised the third day to triumph over death and sin and we too can be sons and daughters with Him.

Read the Authorized Version, King James Bible which is up to date 1990. Jesus while on earth said:

"You must be born again," also "I am the way, the truth and the life. No man cometh to the Father except by me." (John 3:16)

Confess your sins to Jesus, tell him you are sorry from your heart, and He will take away your sins to be remembered against you no more.

**FROM PETER WHITTLEY** *Twickenham, Middlesex*
*5 November 1990*

I believe that we have to face the fact that either there is a God, or there is not.

If there is not, let us eat, drink and be merry, for tomorrow we die – a truly sub-human existence if carried to the extreme. If, on the other hand, there is a God, and the obvious design in the world around us argues strongly for the fact, then we cannot shut our eyes to the evidence. Sir James Jeans, the eminent astronomer, once said that the universe appears to have been made by a pure mathematician.

If we accept the idea of such a God, then we must accept He must be a higher intelligence than ourselves, and that He would want to communicate with his creation.

Christians believe that the Bible is God's self-revelation to mankind, and that His greatest self-revelation is in sending His Son, Jesus Christ, into the world in human form.

By His life, and preeminently by His death and resurrection, God showed Himself to be a God of love, and also a righteous and holy God – a God who could not countenance all the wrong things in our human experience.

But the Bible also tells us that, in a way which we cannot understand, the death and resurrection of Jesus Christ opens a way back to God for all mankind. Our God has given us a free will. We can accept the self-revelation of God and dedicate our lives to Him, or we can reject the whole idea and go our own way, "do our own thing".

Jesus said, "Whoever comes to me, I will never drive away". (John 6:37)

**FROM RUTH WOOD**                    *Plymouth, Devon*
*1 November 1990*

Popular theology has reduced the commandments of Christ and his Apostles to a practical nothing.

. . . Before we can keep the commandments, we must know them, and the only way is to read what God says in the Bible.

Twenty minutes reading each day, with an open mind, gets through the whole of the Old Testament once, and the New Testament twice, in a year.

The first feeling I had doing this was of excitement, reading of the promises God made to Abraham. Genesis 12 onwards goes on to tell us of the return of Jesus to the earth, when the world will be put right.

One of my first verses I came to understand (at age 50 I may say) was Mark 16:16, which says: "He that believeth and is baptized shall be saved."

I knew my parents had had me christened when a baby. How on earth could I have believed anything then? The word "believe" comes first. The understanding of this in my heart led me to being fully immersed in water, and putting on the saving Name of Jesus.

This was my start of trying to please God.

Firmly I believe and truly
God is Three, and God is One.

**I believe . . .**
in the Holy Trinity

FROM BRIAN MORRIS                    *Whitchurch, North Shropshire*
                                                    *14 December 1990*

I believe in God the Father, Creator of the whole of LIFE, in all its many and varied forms.

I believe in God the Son, Redeemer of the whole of LIFE, in all its many and varied forms.

I believe in God the Holy Ghost, the Lover and Sanctifier of the whole of LIFE, in all its many and varied forms.

I cannot understand, comprehend, analyse or begin to assess adequately this TRINITY. I *can* and *do* feel its presence, guidance and influence.

It is the pride of man, and the value he places on his own rationality which has been, and still is, the cause of so much unhappiness and confusion in the world. Man has created his own hell. In his pain and anguish he bites, most viciously, the hand of Love so often extended to him.

It will not be until man comes to realize and accept his gross limitations, that a state of mind approaching serenity (for which millions down the ages have plundered, murdered, and pillaged, often themselves becoming the main victims) will be his.

The final act in his progress towards this blessed

state will be to accept the TRINITY, in HUMILITY and FAITH.

This is what I believe.

**FROM ARTHUR AND DORIS HARVEY**        *Newport, Gwent*
                                        *6 November 1990*

We believe in an Almighty and Holy God, creator of all things, yet He is our Heavenly Father who has infinite love for His children.

We believe in His Son, Jesus, who came to earth to show us what God is like. He died to restore our relationship with God, and He rose from death so that we too might live happy, victorious lives.

We believe in the Holy Spirit, whom God has sent to make Jesus real to us today.

We believe that the Bible is the inspired Word of God, which gives us comfort and direction.

We believe that God answers prayer, and we give Him praise.

We believe that the Church is the company of people, worldwide, who acknowledge that Jesus is Lord and who live in the power given by the Holy Spirit.

We believe that one day – we don't know when – Jesus will return to take His Church, past and present, to be with Him in heaven.

And so we could continue telling of our belief; but, meantime, we live in the joy of it all, and try to share our joy with others. Of course we have our ups and downs like everyone else, but we face all of life with confidence and hope, because of our belief and because of the reality of God, Father, Son and Holy Spirit, who lives in us.

FROM MISS JEAN RADDON *Caterham, Surrey*
*8 April 1991*

God is real. God is one but, like a clover leaf, He has three parts, the Father, the Son and the Holy Spirit. God created all things.

Satan, God's enemy, constantly tries to destroy all God's good works. Adam and Eve, the first created humans, chose to listen to Satan rather than to God.

Consequently their descendants have a natural tendency to break rather than to keep God's laws.

God is just. Lawbreakers must bear their sentence, which is death.

God loves men, and wants them to live, not die. To satisfy His love and His justice, God sent His Son to be a man, and to bear man's death sentence. Jesus never broke God's laws and so was the only person good enough to die in man's place.

God restored Jesus to life on the third day, defeating Satan, who wanted to keep Jesus a captive in death. Jesus showed Himself to His friends after His resurrection of which they are historical witnesses. Forty days later Jesus went back to His Father in Heaven.

We can be assured of a place in heaven by becoming a Christian. This means to believe that Jesus is God's Son, who lived as a man, died in man's place, rose from his tomb and returned to Heaven. It means to confess and ask pardon for sin, and to make Jesus master of our life. The Holy Spirit then abides with us.

FROM MRS M. JOY WILLIAMS *Chorleywood, Hertfordshire*
*5 November 1990*

I believe in God. How can I do any other when I look around me and see all the beauty of this world? It couldn't have happened by accident. There must be a mind, a creative spirit behind the vastness of our awesome universe, and the intricate pattern of snowflakes, each different from any other.

I believe in Jesus, God's Son, sent to earth as a human, to live as we do, to suffer and finally to die for our sakes, that we might comprehend at least a little how much God loves us. We could never have known God as Father were it not for Christ.

I believe in the Holy Spirit. I see Him at work in people's lives wherever there is kindness, generosity, courage and love.

Despite all the suffering, tragedy, cruelty, selfishness and violence; despite my fear for the future of my grandchildren, my country, and the world, yet I still believe that God will not be defeated, and good will triumph over evil.

I believe our life is a spiritual journey which does not end with death, but that our spirit will be released into new dimensions. I believe that when that time comes I will understand so much that puzzles me now.

There are times when faith flickers and fear and doubt creep in, but thank God that He renews my faith, for without it, I would find life dark and hopeless.

FROM HARRY F. NORMAN,
LT. CDR, R.N. (RTD)
                 *Waterlooville, Hampshire*
                 *11 November 1990*

Benjamin Disraeli once said to Bishop Wilberforce: "Man, my Lord, is a being born to believe."

We all believe, and our beliefs, although many and varied, are mostly practical. We are what we believe. Our attitude to life, our motives, our reactions, our loves, our hates, our fears and fancies are all because of what we believe. The area in which belief is of the greatest consequence, impact and effect is that of religious belief. Even an atheist is a believer: he believes there is no God. The greater part of human history has been created by men and women acting upon their religious beliefs.

From the very beginning of Christianity Christians were people with a profound belief in certain things. These beliefs became written down in the third century as the Creed, so called from the Latin *"credo"* "I believe". The Creed, stating what the Bible teaches, became an important test of true Christianity and its effects on daily living.

To believe in God as Father and His only Son as personal Lord and Saviour imparts a comfortable sense of inner peace and security in a very troubled and confused world.

To believe in the Holy Spirit is to believe that God is actively involved in the affairs of men and that good will triumph over evil. The last word will be His.

To believe in the resurrection of the body and the life everlasting as God's own gift of grace is to look upon growing old as merely progress towards a glorious future and to lose fear of death and the grave, seeing them only as stepping stones across the river to a land of eternal delight. In all this I must and do believe.

How sweet the name of Jesus
sounds
In a believer's ear

**I believe . . .**
Jesus saves!

FROM MRS VICKY WAITE

*Isle of Seil, Argyll*
*19 November 1990*

I started to write "I believe" in 250 words – but this
came instead.

I believe that Christ will come again
And I believe He's coming SOON – to reign,
    To judge our weak, rebellious hearts,
    Our good or evil deeds.
    The Prophecies foretell! –
    Yet no-one heeds.

I believe that "something has to give".
We've lost our way – forgotten how to live.
    God made our world
    And showed us how to do it.
    We spurned His laws,
    Went right ahead and blew it.

We need you, Jesus – blessed Son of God
    For time is short and
    Something's *GOT* to give.

FROM MR A. E. JOHNSON *Norwich, Norfolk*
*8 November 1990*

I respond with pleasure to the editor's request headed "I believe".

My wife and I are lifelong Methodists and seldom repeat the Creed, but we do BELIEVE, and especially in the following words – "And in Jesus Christ". For it is in Him and through Him that we are able to reach the Godhead.

Lots of folk today are suffering from stress without realizing the power of prayer and forgiveness. The cure is to have a little talk with Jesus.

We have raised a family of four sons and ten grandchildren and one great grandchild, and we have every reason to believe in Him and Praise Him – Hallelujah!

You see, we are all part of God's family, and Jesus came to show us the Way (not always an easy one) and he says, "Follow me."

FROM MRS MOLLIE BENNETT *Leyland, Lancashire*
*21 November 1990*

I believe in many things, but most of all I believe in Jesus Christ. In our Christian lives we should have a close relationship with Jesus Christ and through Him with God the Father.

Martin Luther once said: "Take hold of Jesus as a man, and you will discover that He is God."

He came to earth in human form at a particular time in history in a particular place. I am sure in His earthly life Jesus worked hard at the ordinary things of life (we can't all be brilliant and clever) but if we believe in Jesus and take Him as our example, there is work for Him that each one of us can do.

When I look at a picture of Jesus and remember my faults and failings, I also remember He loves me and I hope He finds that, amid all my faults and failings, I do believe in Him and try to do His work in quiet and simple places.

Jesus had a great interest in men and women and their affairs. He called himself the "Son of Man" which certainly meant among other things that He belongs not to one family or one race, but to all men for all time.

He comes today as closely to us as He did to His first disciples. He is human and He is divine. The disciples, as they worked and toiled with their Master, believed in His humanity and His divinity, just as we, His disciples today, say and mean:

"Yes, I believe in Jesus Christ."

FROM MR J. A. COLLINS                    *Bournemouth, Dorset*

I have been a believer for the last 63 years. I am now 80 years old. The Christian faith is the one and only way to really understand life and death.

First of all, everyone acknowledges the life and death of Christ by the day and date that we use, BC and AD, which of course, is an historical fact.

Now regarding Jesus Christ, he was either the greatest impostor that ever lived, or, as I and thousands of Christians maintain, he was indeed, as he claimed to be, the very Son of God.

God has revealed himself in several ways through creation, through history, particularly in his dealings with the nation of Israel, and the nations surrounding her, but the greatest revelation of himself is in Christ Jesus . . .

And he is alive today, and he is changing people's

lives, and not only that, he has gone to prepare a place in heaven for all who believe and receive him as Lord and Saviour.

**FROM ROBERT E. HARVEY**     *Bolton, Lancashire*
                                             *15 November 1990*

My faith is based upon the promises of Jesus, because He proved to the world that He keeps His promises. He told His disciples that He would be killed by evil men, but in three days He would return from the grave. They didn't believe Him, but God did raise Him on the third day.

The story of Jesus is not a fairy tale, as the mockers would have us believe. History records that He was born in Bethlehem, spent His childhood with Mary and Joseph, and then in His maturity He went around preaching and teaching. After His resurrection He was taken up into Heaven, watched by His disciples. Jesus lives.

No man, either before or since, has had such an influence on mankind. We have AD and BC in our historical records to confirm it, as well as millions of people who believe in Him. I believe in Jesus because there is such beauty and joy in His teaching, so much hope in His promises.

Jesus said (John 5:24):

"I am telling you the truth: whoever hears my words and believes in Him who sent me has eternal life. He will not be judged, but has already passed from death to life."

I believe.

FROM MRS EVA STEWART          *Billericay, Essex*
*4 November 1990*

In my early twenties, largely through a godly grandmother, I came to know the Lord Jesus Christ personally.

It tells us in the Bible (Acts 16:31):

Believe on the Lord Jesus Christ, and thou shalt be saved.

Saved? From what? Sin, that all of us suffer from; worry, another thing, uncertainty as to what happens after death. Rest is what we obtain, when we come to know Jesus.

It isn't just "religion", it's Jesus, who died for us on the cross. When we give ourselves over to Him He is real to us. I've proved it for nearly 70 years now, must be, I'm now nearly 82. So I would say: read the Bible, especially the Gospels, and find out about Jesus and get to know Him.


FROM GARTH WAITE          *Oban, Argyll*

I believe that the planet I inhabit is unique in the universe, in that it has been visited by the Son of God, and that His promise to visit it again will be fulfilled.

I believe that nothing that is happening in the world today is outside the cognizance of the Almighty, who observes it in the perspective of a perpetual NOW. This is beyond the understanding of inhabitants of space and time.

In other words, I believe that God is not a fascinating uncertainty, but an incomprehensible certainty.

By definition, my belief must be *my own possession*.

No-one can rob me of it, it does not need an insurance policy to protect it, nor is it vulnerable to the ravages of moth or rust.

Furthermore, and most important, I believe that there is more to the Christian faith than a bare assent to the truth of the Bible, acceptance of the creeds or a certificate of confirmation. My unconditional belief is a sure trust in a pardoning God, and that I am reconciled to Him through the blood of the cross.

I have proved in my own experience the promise of the Old Testament prophet:

"They that wait upon the Lord shall renew . . .
their quietness and confidence" –

precious possessions in these days!

FROM MRS JANE YOUNG           *Wollaston, Northamptonshire*
                              *29 December 1990*

Yes, I believe in a Being far beyond my comprehension, who guides and sustains me. Whether as a person I am "right" or "wrong" in the way other people see me, I do not care.

This Being – whom Christians call God, myself included – revealed Himself in the person of Jesus Christ. How this came about does not greatly concern me. He is the epitome of all that I am able to understand about the purpose of living.

My belief was made a certainty 66 years ago when I was confirmed. The "heavens opened" that day, and I knew for sure that for me there is another world, beyond anything we can adequately express in words, or creeds.

Immortal, invisible, God only wise
In light inaccessible, hid from our
eyes

**I believe . . .**
that there, too, truth lies

(Here are some letters from people who believe that
there is much to be said for all world religions, as well
as Christianity, and that perhaps we should be more
open-minded and ready to listen to men and women of
other faiths, even to atheists and humanists – because
they, too, have their point of view.)

FROM MRS DOROTHY WOO

*Sheffield, Yorkshire*
(in Saga, *June 1991*)

My marriage to a man of different race was an unusual
event forty years ago, and not an easy path of life to
choose. Gratitude to God has deepened in me as He
has led me through many difficult times with a Chinese
husband at my side.

My husband became a university lecturer, and we
had the opportunity to meet people of many national-
ities and faiths. Our home was a place where overseas
students and visitors came and went, leaving their
mark.

Through these experiences, along with the joys and
sorrows of everyday living and bringing up children, I
have come to believe that no narrow creed can embrace
truth. Life is a mystery and portions of truth are given

to us as we respond to the spiritual promptings within us.

"The kingdom of God is within you," said Jesus.

That is why prayer is so essential. It is when we draw apart to be quiet with God that His spirit can speak to us and guide us. Worship with fellow Christians, too, is a great source of strength and I am still a devoted Methodist. As we pray and worship, our hearts are softened with compassion and tenderness towards our fellow human beings, animals, birds, plants and the whole of God's creation.

I believe "God is Green" and His will is that the spirit of Christ, which is the spirit of love, should become manifest throughout the Cosmos. In fact Christ's spirit is everywhere, loving and redeeming, but our sin and selfishness separate us from him.

Unlike many Christians, I do not find a sensible concept of reincarnation incompatible with the saving power of Christ. It can be part of a process of evolution. We come back in order to share in the work of redemption. This we can do if we receive into ourselves the power of Christ's love.

FROM MRS MARCIA KIRK                                    *London*

Brought up in the Church of England religion, I found it a source of strength and comfort throughout my life, and like Marjory Davys, I lament the fact that religion seems to be lacking in our modern code of living.

Is it a matter of us not having time, or of using our time in search of material things? This does not appear to be so with Eastern religions. In NW London we have an example of this. A beautiful Hindu Temple, built with volunteer labour and the materials freely given.

When you visit this Temple you are not even asked for a donation.

A few hundred yards down the road there is a magnificent old C. of E. church, which has been converted into flats, for money! Even our cathedrals have shops trading within their walls.

The younger generation tell me that religion is "old hat" and science has proved this, but has it? The more I read of scientific discoveries, the more credible I find some parts of the Bible. (e.g., the walls of Jerico being brought down by trumpets – "Subsonic, maybe?" Eric von Dineken gives food for thought in his books like *We are not the first*.)

Perhaps we should get on the modern wavelength and point out the parallel between science and religion. After all, we have been mistakenly thinking that conformation to God's will is not necessary since the days of Adam and Eve.

Will we never learn?

FROM MRS DILYS ELLIOTT                    *Portsmouth, Dorset*
                                          *29 January 1991*

I believe that everyone has the right to their own Faith or philosophy, as long as it is not imposed on others. Among *Saga*'s many club members and clientele must be those of different religions or, as I am, agnostic, belonging to the British Humanist Association.

I hope, therefore, that "I believe" will not be an outlet only for the Christian faith.

FROM MRS CYNTHIA CASTELLAN      *Rugeley, Staffordshire*
*21 February 1991*

When I was attending a multi-cultural school at Haifa (Israel) in 1935, my father, a devout Christian, said I must understand that our God was worshipped by other people.

"The Jews, you know about," he said, "but do remember He is also Allah. The Mahommedan (the term then used for 'Muslim') says that Allah is God and Mahomet was his Prophet."

But what was acceptable to a child was far harder in later life, when the Gulf War started. It seemed impossible to pray for anybody, though I found I could when I remembered the words of St Chrysostom:

"Fulfil now, O Lord, the desires and petitions of Thy servants *as may be most expedient for them.*"

FROM MRS MARY PEARCE      *Truro, Cornwall*
*30 December 1990*

I believe in reincarnation. Having been dedicated (christened) in the Salvation Army, through childhood I graduated to the Elim Foursquare Gospel Church, Assemblies of God, Apostolic Church, Baptist Church and "Other denominations" through my service in the WAAF, and after the War, Church of England. After much heart-searching I now firmly believe that God is Life itself, and not a person in human form tucked away somewhere.

J. TEAPE                    *Walton, Felixstowe, Suffolk*

I believe that light is an essential attribute of God. There are many references to it in the Bible:

"The Lord is my light and my salvation."

"God is light and in him is no darkness at all."

The other great world religions make reference to it as well. In the sacred Scriptures of Islam, the Koran, we find:

"God is the light of the heavens and the earth."

This love of light has universally captured the imagination of man. Our pagan ancestors saw the sun as the centre of their devotions: the eternal and unchanging light. Hidden in mystery at times, reflected at night through the moon, it remained behind all life, giving warmth and strength to man and beast. It was felt and worshipped always and ever, not just on Sunday in best clothes: a simple, but unifying thought.

When we speak of God as light, we do not always realize how apt the metaphor is. The darkness makes everything shapeless and strange. With the coming light, the infinite complexity of the details of life are clearly revealed.

Light, in its universality, has many shapes and forms: firelight, torchlight, candle light, electric light, and all fashioned for different purposes. The difference between the glory of the sun and the flickering candle is only one of degree.

We know what light we can bear. Many people find their light in Jesus, who carries the measure of the godhead their souls can bear. Some find light in Buddha or Muhammad, others in their fellows or family: differing forms, differing measures, different names. We cannot say, because I get my light from electricity, my neighbour has no light because he uses an oil lamp. The source is the same: the light universal from which all flows.

So, in our acknowledgement of the source of the divine light, we should acknowledge the insights of others, even though their preferred light may not be ours. In the words of Hindu Scripture, the Bhagavad-Gita:

> He who seeth me everywhere and seeth every-thing in me, of him will I never lose hold, and he will never lose hold of me. He who, established in serenity, worshippeth me abiding in all things, that man cometh to me, whatever his mode of existence.

FROM MRS MADELINE CLEAVER   *Aylesbury, Buckinghamshire*
*14 November 1990*

I believe – but not always completely – in the Christian religion. I am a very regular churchgoer and am really involved with my church, really enjoy the fellowship as well as the services and other activities, and the way the caring attitude of people is demonstrated. That said, I still have doubts; I am still questioning and believe that people who never doubt, who never question the precepts of their faith, tend to be narrow in their views.

Non-churchgoers will often say: "There are as good people who never go to church as there are who do." They are right, and I would go further, there are some better people – but not usually the people who put the point. The people who talk like that are usually uncomfortably justifying their non-churchgoing, so perhaps they have a need, only half-admitted to themselves. It is not my belief that all those who do not go to church are unworthy in some way – perhaps they do have a very real faith and do a great deal of good but have made a conscious decision, having thought deeply, that going to church is not for them.

When I go to church and take the Eucharist, I do at least pray that I am sincere in what I am doing, whatever my doubts, and that my efforts to live a good and unselfish life may be successful to some degree.

I believe that whether everything in the Bible is true or not, whether, even, there is any truth in the basic Christian religion or not, the true way of Christianity is a good way to live. But it may not be the only way.


FROM CHARLES WARD                    *Stroud, Gloucestershire*

I have no wish to be captious, since the views already expressed in this column broadly reflect caring, tolerant and idealistic attitudes. Such can only be commended at any age. Yet there is one thing that troubles me.

The title "I believe" might be deemed to exclude the many agnostics sure to be numbered among *Saga* magazine readers. Those who describe themselves as agnostics, humanists and the like may be just as caring, tolerant and idealistic as those who affirm their various beliefs.

However, their experience of life, on which many have reflected with no less intensity than the religious, has led them to refrain from making assertions of belief concerning matters which, though pleasing to contemplate, or which are poetic or inspiring, lie beyond incontrovertible demonstration or proof.

Humane, moral and progressive concepts are not the prerogative of the pious, although this is frequently assumed. To admit limitations of human knowledge does not prevent one from being a happy, loving, responsible person.

I believe we should stop making such a fuss over what I, or you, believe.

What are we actually doing? Usually we are merely making a number of assertions which no-one is able to substantiate. Statements that are not self-evident, and neither rationally nor scientifically verifiable. Nothing more, when you come to the crunch, than expressions of personal hopes and desires . . .

Are we still children whose sorrows and difficulties must be soothed away? Must we be cajoled into being "good" through being given expectations of reward?

Can we not, after all our years in this world, all our observation of and delight in the variety of human experience, keep a child's sense of wonder, but attain a mature appraisal of what is actually known, and what lies beyond our knowing?

FROM PHILIP SCHOFIELD *Lowsonford, Warwickshire*
*31 October 1990*

"I believe in God . . ." are the first four words of the Creed used in Christian churches. No doubt they could be used by those of other beliefs. When I joined the Indian Army in the last war, at the age of 21, I was living with Hindus, Sikhs and Muslims, which made me face up to the questions: who has the truth?

By chance I found in a back-street bazaar a book on

comparative religion written by Bishop Gore, describing all known religions of the world. One sentence struck me then, and has remained with me ever since. He wrote:

> Only one man has ever lived who claimed to be one with God Almighty, and hasn't finished up in a lunatic asylum.

*I believe* in God and in Jesus Christ, who died and rose again and appeared to many of his followers (of which there is ample evidence) and promises us love and joy and peace eternal if we follow him.

I believe, too, that the obscene horrors in Northern Ireland, alleged to be committed by Catholic Christians against Protestant Christians, and by Protestant Christians against their Roman Catholic brothers, must be utterly repugnant to God –

"My command is that you shall love one another."

And with the dawn,
those angel faces smile
That I have loved long since;
and lost awhile.

## I believe . . .
in everlasting life

This is our last section: what people believe about eternity. For some it was the experience of bereavement that led them into belief about an afterlife.

I get so many sad letters on *Praise Be!* from people who have lost someone very dear to them – and they say that they can't believe they will ever get over it. And so I would like to include here something I said on my last series of *Praise Be!*, which is my own belief about why we have to bear such great pain at bereavement, and how we do manage to get over it.

**FROM THORA HIRD**
*London*
*17 August 1992*

I believe that when you lose someone you love very much, it feels as though you're carrying a big heavy brick in your chest. Your heart just aches and aches with the weight of this brick.

I imagine the Lord giving us that brick – it's the weight of all the love we shared. Because you wouldn't want to just feel *nothing*, would you?

And very, very gradually the brick fades away at the edges. You don't notice at first, and it may take years, but one day you're left with just the loving, happy memories, and your heart is light again.

I know, because I've carried one of those bricks – more than once. But the heavy bricks that came into my heart when my mother died, far too young, and my sister Olga, in a road accident, my brother Neville, of cancer, and my dad – have all melted away now. I still love and miss them all – but the bricks have gone.

FROM MRS E. M. RAWLINGS                    *Chelmsford, Essex*

When my mother died I found myself praying each night that I might see her – just once more. But I did not.

Then, one night, she did come, not as I had known her, but as a young woman, dressed in long dark skirt and white blouse. I realized that this was how my father might well have thought of her, and I knew that she had not come before because she was with him.

I used to travel to Kent to see him each Friday and, about a year later, my mother came to me again one Tuesday night. In the morning, I told my husband that my mother wanted me to go to my father. I got the earliest train and went down to find that he had not been feeling well, was worried and depressed. I was able to sort things out and leave him in a happier frame of mind.

My father died some years ago and, although I have not seen my mother again, I do not need to. Now I do not just "believe" in the life everlasting – I know.

FROM MRS MARLYS PEARCE *Worthing, West Sussex*

The more of my greatly loved older family and friends who die, the more I believe in a life beyond death.

I arrived at my mother's hospital bedside half an hour after she had gone. She had had four years of a weakening illness. As I knelt beside her body, upset at not being with her at the end, the clearest thought came into my mind. It was just as though she was still in the room.

"Don't grieve for me. I am in the place of perfect health, perfect peace and perfect joy."

This, and other similar experiences, have helped me to know that our souls go on living. I think that our short human lives are a preparation for our life in the world to come.

I believe at the time of our dying we shall meet Absolute Love. In that Presence will all our doubts and fears be seen as mere shadows, and all our hurts be healed. I believe, because that Love is most merciful, we may be given a last chance to be sorry for the many things we have done against Love's spirit of Absolute Truth and Purity, and for the attitudes and prejudices we have held which have hurt other people.

I believe also that in this next life – as we allow our spirits to be made whole – we shall, in some way, have an ongoing part to play in the eternal battle between good and evil in the world.

FROM MRS R. WILLIS *Ashford, Middlesex*
*5 March 1991*

Passing a text on a church notice board recently, I was reminded of the times when my husband helped me, when he referred to "the wisdom of those little wayside pulpits".

During a holiday at Falmouth with him and our grandson, we visited the little church of St Just-in-Roseland, situated in one of the loveliest settings imaginable. It was Eastertime. No church in England has a garden more enchanting. A riot of colour is seen in the varieties of polyanthus growing among the myrtles, hydrangeas, palms and bamboo.

Passing through the picturesque lych-gate, I read this verse on the wall:

Here rest the silent dead, and here too I
When younder dial shall strike the hour, must lie.
Look around! In orderly array
See where the buried hosts await the judgement day.
Stranger, in peace pursue thine onward road,
But ne'er forget thy last and long abode.

I looked at my husband and wondered how I would cope without him, or he without me, a fact which all caring people must face at some time or another . . .

I had seven more years with my considerate man, this compassionate soul who was always willing to help. What among the gems of wisdom shall I quote? Let it be the Easter message of hope to all bereaved:

"I am the resurrection and the life;
he that believeth in me, though he were
    dead,
yet shall he live;
and whosoever liveth and believeth in me
shall never die."

FROM ROBERT J. COOK, M.A.     *East Grinstead, West Sussex*
*16 January 1991*

I am a widower, approaching the new "expectation" of three score years and twenty. It is now five years since my wife died.

Our married life, which had spanned nearly 50 years, had been a very happy and a very active one. In a remark made by Clare Hollingworth to her interviewer (*Saga* magazine, October 1990) I found tremendous encouragement:

"A marriage as happy as that gives you the strength to go on afterwards."

This is a very positive attitude to bereavement. Carrying on with the activities that were begun with a partner who has passed on is, I believe, a very positive way of saying "Thank you" to that partner.

FROM MRS JESSICA WHITE     *Christchurch, Dorset*
*6 November 1990*

No one is born perfect, and as each day passes we are that much nearer death. It is the one thing in life of which we can be absolutely certain, yet never come to terms with.

But does it really matter whether we are convinced of eternity? We can do nothing about it. God, if he exists, did not intend us to spend our entire life worrying about it. I believe He expects us to do the best we can, and if we do not, does He not "forgive us our trespasses"?

On losing my husband some years ago, I received

advice from all and sundry, but it was from my young son that I found peace when I cried:

"Shall we ever see him again?"

"If we do, we shall be overjoyed", came his calm reply. "If not, and there is nothing else, he didn't know, nor shall we. It's as simple as that."

So often we wonder, "Do I believe in God?" Would it not be more pertinent to ask, "Does God believe in me?"

FROM MS EILEEN WILLIAMS          *Tenby, Dyfed*
*7 November 1990*

Most of us were brought up with religious dogma requiring our blind faith. We were not encouraged to seek our own truth, or to question what we were told.

All religions have split into various sects, each believing that only they have the true answers. This has resulted in religious wars and conflicts. Today Arab is against Jew, Muslim against Hindu, Catholic against Protestant, and Jehovah's Witnesses claim they will inherit the earth – and no doubt many will wish them luck with it!

Any independent seeker will discover the Light of Truth hidden under the bushel of the whole gamut of religious belief. The Force of Life IS – call it God or Allah if you wish – but that it exists and permeates all matter, both seen and unseen, is something everyone can agree upon. It is a unifying principle. When it withdraws itself from dense matter (death) it still exists in matter of lesser density. It cannot cease, for IT IS.

Those who have clinically died and have been resuscitated have spoken of life in another dimension but without physical form. Our future is certain, so we give our love and gratitude to that Life Force for giving us the opportunity TO BE. It is up to us to show our worthiness.

Our joy is in knowing "I AM THAT I AM" – "God" is always with us.

FROM MRS JOANNE GORDON JONES          *Salcombe, Devon*

I believe that when we die we will all go into Limbo – a sorting house – where we will be shown what spiritual values really are. Here, I think, we make our choice – belief or disbelief – and I think that only believers will inherit the Kingdom of Heaven. That is why I am so sad for my children, who do not believe.

I feel the presence of my mother and father continually, and look forward to being reunited with them and my son and friends, but I shall not feel so confident of meeting my children when it comes to my turn to cross over into that mysterious life everlasting. I do, of course, pray daily that they may have their eyes opened to the fact that GOD IS.

Our materialist world is so insulated from the spiritual world, and greed is an octopus which strangles our spirits.

I believe that love and suffering are the two most important things in the world, and that we cannot have love without suffering. If we could all learn to give rather than to take what a different place this beautiful world would be . . . and it is so easy.

Apart from "giving", another unpopular word in our society is "discipline", without which we are lost indeed, and why is this such a hard lesson to learn?

Lastly, I believe with Pascal that "all the evils of life have fallen upon us because men will not sit alone quietly in a room." So many of us are afraid of being alone, so many are afraid of silence. There is so much noise in our world, and everyone in such a hurry – for what?

**FROM GINA WILLIAMS**                    *Barmouth, Gwynedd*
                                                *2 November 1990*

I have never been influenced by superstitious or evangelical blandishments, nor have I found peace during church services, although I have many times found it in the singular atmosphere of a churchyard.

It does not disturb me to consider that death will be the end: why should I exist after death any more than I did before conception? Life seems random, fleeting and inexplicable. That it must end at death I believe to be logical.

This does not mean that we should spend these brief moments of life in aimless pursuits. A reward in itself is the constant search for Love and Truth, even if it leads to the acceptance of the idea of Nothingness which is, after the uncertainties and anxieties of our brief existence, the only real conclusion – the eternal peace.

**FROM E. G. H. CROUCH**        *Knaresborough, North Yorkshire*
                                           *24 December 1990*

I do not expect an existence after this one; for me, this is the only life I shall know. But that does not mean that for me, and many others like myself, that life is cold and without beauty or has no significance. On the contrary, I take as much pleasure in a glorious sunset as anyone else; for me the symphonies of Mozart and Beethoven seem like miracles, and life has as much meaning as we choose to give it. The *meaning* of life is something we invest it with.

For me a sense of satisfaction comes from accepting that there are some things which we can know with certainty, and others on which it is idle to speculate. We can each, in our own individual way, enjoy and take delight in the world, with all its diversity and wonder, and take pleasure in this life without expecting anything beyond.

FROM MRS CAROLINE V. BARNES    *Crowborough, East Sussex*
*12 November 1990*

I believe. At age 81 and alone, these two words have great meaning. A belief seems to come from within oneself as truth. As one nears passing on, my own belief becomes stronger, and I cannot think it will change.

I *do* believe that the essence of all life as we know it goes on and is indestructable, and comes from one great source.

I believe in reincarnation, and that at some time I shall have another chance to experience and learn the next phase of being, as another person.

I have no religious creeds, but am thankful for all the varied experiences of my long life, the good, the bad, the love of other humans and the love of animals.

*None of us knows* what awaits us. Each of us *hopes*. Should there be nothing at the end, we have had the joy of hope. Should there be life, we shall have the joy of living.

I believe in a future. I also believe in prayer, one of which is that my beloved pets will pass over naturally before it is my turn. In the meantime, *this* life is great!

**FROM MR PATRICK JOHN TYSON**                    *Stowmarket, Suffolk*
                                                  *25 November 1990*

I am an ex-serviceman aged 61.

When we say we are facing eternity, we should always remember that although this life sometimes seems bare, dark and frequently painful, this is only a part of our soul's journeying. I believe this journey began a long time ago, before birth. Our life and death are merely stages in a continuous process.

During life we are conditioned to deny our intuitive faith in our immortality. It is for this reason we are afraid of death, because we only know what happens to our flesh when the fire burns and the knife cuts, even though these are part of life, not death.

On the day when answers to these mysteries are revealed, all our preconceived ideas, like our possessions, will be left behind. We will be faced, at last, with the same truth that our forefathers and mothers were aware of before us. It is then we will say, "What a fool I have been! Was there no limit to my self-importance?" And at last we will return to the continuing journey of our souls.

Therefore, I say, do not be afraid, even though the soul is often surrounded by God's protective darkness. In death will come a knowledge of him which is greater than any imagined before.

FROM MRS EDNA MATTHEWS *Rhyl, Clwyd*

## *Rebirth*

Death is being born again, not the end of our
existence,
An experience we all go through, most with great
resistance!

As a babe content in his mother's womb
We resist the pulls of birth –
Do not want to leave this home
To start again on earth.

But the pains of birth are soon dispelled as he sees his
mother's face
Knows he is safe, protected, loved, will be happy in
this place.

So life goes on, and with it comes its shares of joys
and sorrow,
Then gradually the fears of death bring dread of the
last tomorrow.
Why should we fear the thought of death? It's just
another stage,
Another life to which we pass, the turning of a page.

FROM TED PICK *Stone, Staffordshire*
*5 November 1990*

Thirty years ago an event occurred which changed my
life.
  I went to the dentist to have a tooth extracted with

the use of gas. Breathing in the gas, I suddenly found myself staring and unable to move, but still conscious. At the next instant I found myself watching the scene from behind, apparently from the rear top corner of the room. Looking from behind, I saw every move the dentist made – adjusting the valves behind the chair, and leaning over twice to raise an eyelid and peer into an eye.

These events subsequently proved to be completely factual, although there was no physical way I could have seen them. At the time I was convinced that I had died in the chair.

I am an "earthy" male, who has had no other spiritual or psychic experience. But because I have been "outside of my body", I am convinced that I shall continue to exist after physical death.

I believe each of us has a purpose on earth, that we are here to learn lessons and to improve ourselves, and that probably we shall be required to review our actions eventually.

I think it is likely that most people have to live more than one life during the course of their learning process. When I was young I thought of death as "the last great adventure". Now I am 65, although in no hurry to pass over, I believe it could be my NEXT great adventure!

FROM MRS D. J. THOMSON                    *Edinburgh*

I believe that when we die, we are greeted by our loved ones. Our animal friends are there also – they too have been waiting for us. We shall be renewed, in that we shall not suffer from life's infirmities, the deaf shall hear, the dumb talk, the lame walk, and the blind shall see.

We shall have homes where we can be with our dear ones. Lovely surroundings, too, gardens, fields, rivers and hills. The next world will be very like our present one, otherwise we would not feel at home, would we? But it will be more beautiful than we could ever imagine.

There will be opportunities to learn things we have been unable to learn in this life – Halls of Learning and of Music. We shall be able, later on, to advance to more evolved worlds, but this will take ages. It will be enough for a very long time just to be again with those we love.

I believe all normal decent people can look forward to this sort of world, regardless of creed. I am sure God has no favourites. I do not believe in a Hell of fire and brimstone, but I believe that really wicked people go to a very different type of place, where they must stay until they have changed sufficiently to feel remorse for their sins, and where they must make some sort of atonement.

All this, I believe.

FROM MISS E. A. ODELL                              *Leicester*

I am in my seventies and in reasonable health, but as I look at the obituary columns of our local paper, and frequently see the names of my contemporaries, I realize that one day my name will be there.

It is a sobering thought, yet I do not believe that it is God's will for me to spend my time bemoaning the past, or speculating about the future. Rather, I should try to live my life from day to day under his guidance, and I can testify to the way in which he has strengthened and upheld me, forgiven me when I have gone astray and enabled me to make a fresh start.

I do not know the answer to many questions about the hereafter. Shall I recognize loved ones who have gone before? Shall I know what is happening to those I have left behind?

What I do know is the promise of Jesus:

"I go to prepare a place for you" (John 14:2, 3)

and because he has kept so many promises during my lifetime, I cannot doubt that he will keep this final promise. So I have nothing to fear.

When I go on a *Saga* holiday, I am always relieved to see a courier waiting at the station to escort me on the last stage of my journey.

When I reach the end of life's pilgrimage, I believe that He who has been my earthly guide will be waiting to take me into his Father's presence.

## *Just as I Am*

Just as I am, without one plea
But that they Blood was shed for me,
And that thou bidd'st me come to thee,
O Lamb of God, I come.

Just as I am, though tossed about
With many a conflict, many a doubt,
Fightings within, and fears without,
O Lamb of God, I come.

Just as I am, poor, wretched, blind;
Sight, riches, healing of the mind,
Yea all I need, in thee to find,
O Lamb of God, I come.

Just as I am, thou wilt receive,
Wilt welcome, pardon, cleanse, relieve:
Because thy promise I believe,
O Lamb of God, I come.

Just as I am (thy love unknown
Has broken every barrier down),
Now to be thine, yea, thine alone,
O Lamb of God, I come.

Just as I am, of that free love
The breadth, length, depth, and height to prove,
Here for a season, then above,
O Lamb of God, I come.

CHARLOTTE ELLIOTT (1789–1871)